Revision Notes
for
National 5
Chemistry

D A Buchanan
**(Moray House School of Education,
University of Edinburgh)**

J R Melrose
(formerly Lenzie Academy)

Published by
Chemcord
Inch Keith
East Kilbride
Glasgow

ISBN 87057091X

© Buchanan and Melrose, 2013

Printed by Bell and Bain Ltd, Glasgow

Note to students

The course

- This book is designed to cover all of the essential content of the National 5 Chemistry Course as well as the content of the National 4 Chemistry Course that is judged to be helpful for progression to National 5.
- Content of National 4 Course for which there is no obvious progression to National 5 is included as background information and indicated with ✶✶✶. This material does **not** have to be revised for the National 5 examination.
- Information that may be of use to you can be found in the Data Booklet. A copy of the Data Booklet can be downloaded from the SQA website.
  (www.sqa.org.uk/files_ccc/ChemistryDataBookletSQPN5.pdf).

Your revision

- You are more likely to benefit from your revision if you work at a steady rate and have a study plan.
- You can indicate your knowledge of each statement with a ✓ in the ☐ at the left hand side.
- You can also mark statements with a highlighter pen.
- If there is some part of the course that you do **not** understand, ask your teacher.
- A lot of calculations in the National 5 Chemistry course involve simple proportion. Check with your mathematics or chemistry teacher if you are unsure of the layout used in this book. Key formulae (relationships) are given in the Data Booklet on page three.
- The tests in "*Assessment Tests for National 5 Chemistry*" will check that you have mastered the various parts of a topic and help you pin-point areas of difficulty.
- You can practise examination-type questions using "*Revision Questions for National 5 Chemistry*". This is a useful way of checking that you have really understood the topic and can apply your knowledge and problem solving skills.

Index

Chemical Changes and Structure

Nature's Chemistry

Chemistry in Society

1 Rate of reactions

Different rates

☐ Chemical reactions do **not** all occur at the same rate; some are over in a fraction of a second (fast) while others can take years (slow); most reactions occur at rates between these two extremes (medium).

☐ In the lab:

Reaction	Rate
acid/alkali	fast
acid/chalk	medium
iron/oxygen	slow

☐ Everyday reactions:

Reaction	Rate
gas explosion	fast
making toast	medium
oil forming	slow

Changing the rate

(a) Particle size/surface area

☐ The rate of a chemical reaction increases as the particle size decreases,

e.g. calcium carbonate powder reacts faster with dilute acid than calcium carbonate lumps.

☐ The surface area is related to particle size ... as the particle size decreases, the surface area of reactant particles increases; the new surfaces give more opportunities for collisions (or 'bumps') between reactant particles.

solid particle

cut into two pieces

new surfaces exposed

(b) Concentration

☐ The rate of a chemical reaction decreases as the concentration decreases,

e.g. when an acid is diluted, the rate of reaction between the acid and magnesium decreases.

☐ As concentration decreases, there are fewer opportunities for 'bumps' and so the reaction rate decreases.

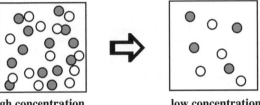

high concentration
of reactants

low concentration
of reactants

☐ With gases, pressure is a measure of the concentration; the rate of reaction of gases in industry is increased by increasing the pressure of the reactants.

(c) Temperature

☐ The rate of a chemical reaction increases as the temperature increases,

e.g. copper burns (reacts with oxygen) when heated but it does not react with oxygen to any extent at room temperature.

☐ The increase in the rate of a chemical reaction with increasing temperature cannot be explained by 'more bumps' (because reactants are moving faster at the higher temperature); the 'bumps' must have a critical level of energy before a reaction will take place,

e.g. nitrogen and oxygen of the air do not begin to react to form oxides of nitrogen even with a large increase in temperature.

☐ As a rough guide, the rate of reaction doubles for every increase in temperature by 10 ºC.

☐ Everyday examples of changing the rate:

   * There is a risk of explosions in coal mines and flour mills since the dust particles are very small (large surface area).

   * Bacterial action on food in a freezer is slower than in a fridge (lower temperature).

   * When air is blown on a fire, the fire burns brighter (higher concentration of oxygen).

Catalysts

☐ **Catalysts** are special substances that can be used to increase the rate of chemical reactions; different reactions require different catalysts.

☐ Catalysts do take part in reactions ... they provide an 'easy route' from reactants to products.

☐ The 'amount' of catalyst at the end of the reaction is the same as at the start, i.e. the catalyst is **not** used up in the reaction; if need be, the catalyst can be recovered chemically unchanged at the end of reaction.

☐ Catalysts are extensively used in the chemical industry; the increased rate of reaction makes the production more profitable,

   e.g. an iron catalyst is used in the manufacture of ammonia.

☐ A catalyst is found in a catalytic converter, fitted to the exhaust systems of cars to convert harmful gases to harmless gases.

☐ An **enzyme** is a biological catalyst ... they catalyse the reactions taking place in the living cells of plants and animals,

   e.g. amylase in the breakdown of starch during digestion.

☐ Enzymes are also important in industrial processes,

   e.g. zymase in yeast in the manufacture of alcohol.

Following the course of a reaction

☐ As a chemical reaction proceeds, reactants are being used up while products are being formed; the rate at which this happens can be followed by measuring the change in a 'property' of a substance involved in the reaction over a period of time,

   e.g. in the reaction of calcium carbonate with dilute hydrochloric acid, carbon dioxide gas is given off.

   $$CaCO_3 \text{ (s)} \quad + \quad HCl \text{ (aq)} \quad \longrightarrow \quad CaCl_2 \text{ (aq)} \quad + \quad H_2O \text{ (l)} \quad + \quad CO_2 \text{ (g)}$$

☐ The change in mass with time (due to gaseous product) can be measured using a balance; the gas produced can be collected using a measuring cylinder or syringe and the volume of gas measured with time.

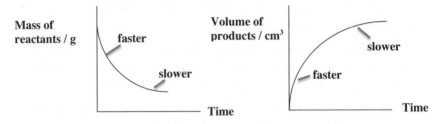

☐ The reaction rate is most rapid at the start of the reaction and decreases as the reaction proceeds.

☐ The steeper the slope, the faster the rate of reaction.

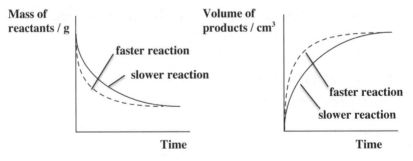

☐ Special probes can also be used to measure changes in other properties,

   e.g. concentration and pH.

☐ The shorter the time for a particular change to take place, the faster the rate of reaction, i.e. rate is inversely proportional to time:

$$\text{rate} \ = \frac{1}{t}$$

Average rate of reaction

☐ The **average rate of reaction** can be defined as the measured change divided by the time taken for this change:

$$\text{average rate of reaction} \quad = \quad \frac{\textbf{measured change}}{\textbf{time taken for the change}}$$

☐ The table shows units for average rate of reaction when the time is expressed in seconds.

Measured change	Unit
Mass of reactants / g	$g\,s^{-1}$ (or g/s)
Volume of gas produced / cm^3	$cm^3\,s^{-1}$ (or cm^3/s)
Concentration / $mol\,l^{-1}$ (or mol/l)	$mol\,l^{-1}\,s^{-1}$ (or mol/l/s)

Example 1:
Calculate the average rate of reaction over the first 20 s.

$$\frac{\text{change in mass}}{\text{time}} \ = \ \frac{0.75 - 0.25}{20}$$

$$= \ \frac{0.5}{20}$$

$$= \ \textbf{0.025 g s}^{-1}$$

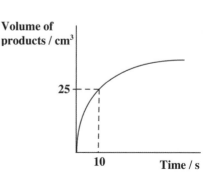

Example 2:
Calculate the average rate of reaction over the first 10 s.

$$\frac{\text{change in volume}}{\text{time}} \ = \ \frac{25 - 0}{10}$$

$$= \ \textbf{2.5 cm}^3\textbf{s}^{-1}$$

2 Elements and compounds

Elements

☐ **Elements** are the building blocks of all the substances in the world just as letters are the building blocks of all the words in our language.

☐ Most elements are solid at room temperature and two are liquid (mercury and bromine).

☐ A property of a substance is something about the substance that is worth knowing … so that the substance can be used in particular ways,

e.g. copper is a good conductor of electricity and so is used in electrical wires; aluminium has a low density and does not corrode easily and so is used to make the bodies of planes.

☐ Although the properties of an element largely determine its use, other things must also be considered,

e.g. gold does not corrode but no manufacturer is going to make cars from gold.

Chemical symbols

☐ A chemical symbol is a shorthand way of representing an element; each has its own chemical symbol.

☐ Modern symbols for elements consist of one or two letters; the first letter is always a capital letter; if there is a second letter, it is always a small letter,

e.g. O for oxygen, Al for aluminium and Cl for chlorine.

☐ A few elements have symbols that come from the Latin name for the element,

e.g. Fe (from ferrum) for iron.

The Periodic Table

☐ All the elements are arranged in a chart called the Periodic Table.

☐ Over 90 elements are found in the ground or in the atmosphere; scientists have been able to make new elements that otherwise would not exist and there are now over 100 known elements.

☐ The modern Periodic Table in use today is not very different from the one drawn up by a Russian chemist called Dmitri Mendeleev; when he arranged the elements in order of increasing 'weight of atom' he noticed that elements with similar chemical properties appeared at regular intervals, i.e. 'periodically' and this is why the arrangement is called the Periodic Table.

☐ He used this observation to form columns, with chemically-like elements placed one below the other.

Each row in the modern Periodic Table is called a **period.**

The vertical columns are called **groups** (or families).

Groups

Period →

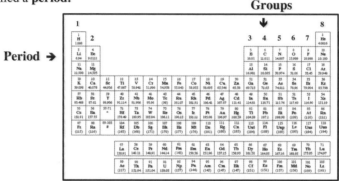

☐ The metals are found to the left-hand side of the Periodic Table and the non-metals (including gases) to the right.

☐ The elements made by scientists are found at the bottom after uranium, *e.g. einsteinium.*

☐ The transition metals lie between Groups 2 and 3, *e.g. iron.*

☐ The Group 1 elements are known as the **alkali metals**; these elements are very reactive and so are stored under oil.

☐ The Group 7 elements are known as the **halogens**.

- [ ] The Group 8 elements are known as the **noble gases**; these are very unreactive (inert) elements.

- [ ] The early Periodic Table had only seven groups because the noble gases were as then undiscovered.

- [ ] All the elements in the one group show very similar chemical properties; down a group there is a trend in physical properties, *e.g. melting and boiling points.*

- [ ] With only a few elements discovered at the time there were gaps in the early Periodic Table; Mendeleev was able to predict the properties of the yet to be discovered elements, *e.g. germanium.*

What are elements made up of?

- [ ] Everything that exists is made up of **atoms**; an element is the simplest type of substance and is made up of atoms of only one kind (but see notes on isotopes on page 14).

- [ ] When scientists make new elements they make new kinds of atoms.

- [ ] Each element has atoms with an **atomic number**; an element can be defined as a collection of atoms all with the same atomic number.

- [ ] Elements are arranged in the Periodic Table in order of increasing atomic number; a new period begins when an element has similar chemical properties to the other elements in Group 1.

- [ ] The mass of an atom is measured on the **relative atomic mass** scale; since this is a relative scale, it has no units; the relative atomic mass for some elements is shown on page 7 of the Data Booklet.

Compounds

☐ A **compound** is a substance that is made up of two or more elements that are chemically joined together; compounds are made from at least two different kinds of atom.

☐ Since they are joined together, it is difficult to separate out the elements that make up the compound ... energy must be supplied to do this,

  e.g. silver oxide can be broken up into silver and oxygen by heat energy, electrical energy can be used to break up copper chloride solution.

☐ A compound is very different from the elements that make it up,

  e.g. sugar (a white solid) is made from carbon (a black solid) and hydrogen and oxygen (both colourless gases); salt (another white solid) is made up of sodium (a very reactive metal) and chlorine (a poisonous green gas).

Naming of compounds

☐ Compounds containing only two elements have names ending in –**ide**,

  e.g. hydrogen oxide is made up only of hydrogen and oxygen.

☐ Compounds containing more than two elements, one of which is oxygen, have names ending in –ate or –ite,

  e.g. calcium nitrate is made up of calcium, nitrogen and oxygen; sodium sulphite is made up of sodium, sulphur and oxygen.

☐ There are exceptions to the –ide rule:
  * When the second part of the name is 'hydroxide', the compound contains hydrogen and oxygen as well as the element in the first part of the name,

  e.g. sodium hydroxide contains sodium, hydrogen and oxygen.

  * When the first part of the name is 'ammonium', the compound contains hydrogen and nitrogen as well as the element in the second part of the name,

  e.g. ammonium chloride contains nitrogen, hydrogen and chlorine.

3 Atomic structure

What are atoms made up of?

☐ Atoms themselves consist of even smaller particles (sub-atomic particles); the way in which the sub-atomic particles are arranged is referred to as the structure of the atom.

☐ At the centre of the atom is a very small 'core' called the **nucleus**.

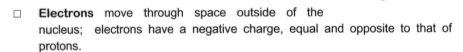

☐ **Protons** are found in the nucleus; protons have a positive charge; this gives a positive charge to the nucleus.

☐ **Electrons** move through space outside of the nucleus; electrons have a negative charge, equal and opposite to that of protons.

☐ **Neutrons** are also found in the nucleus; neutrons do not have a charge, i.e. they are neutral.

☐ Atoms are overall neutral, i.e. they are neither positive nor negative; this means that the total positive charge of the protons in the nucleus is equal to the total negative charge of the electrons.

☐ The masses of the sub-atomic particles are measured on the atomic mass scale; on this scale, protons and neutrons have a mass of one atomic mass unit (amu); compared to protons and neutrons, even on this scale, electrons have almost no mass.

☐ The table shows the mass, charge and location of the sub-atomic particles.

	Mass	**Charge**	**Location**
Proton	1 amu	+	nucleus
Neutron	1 amu	zero	nucleus
Electron	almost zero	−	outside nucleus

Electron arrangement

☐ Electrons are arranged in **shells** (**energy levels**); there is a limit to the number of electrons each shell can hold.

☐ The **first** shell (nearest the nucleus) can hold **2** electrons.

The **second** shell can hold **8** electrons.

The **third** shell can hold **8** electrons (for the first twenty elements).

☐ Electrons always enter the shell in which there is space; this is the shell nearest the nucleus.

Example 1:
lithium (atomic number 3)
has 3 electrons arranged 2, 1

Example 2
chlorine (atomic number 17)
has 17 electrons arranged 2, 8, 7

☐ The electron arrangements of atoms of elements is given are page 1 of the Data Booklet.

☐ All the atoms of elements in the one group have the same number of electrons in the outer shell,

e.g. one electron for all the atoms of the alkali metals.

☐ The chemical reactions of an element depend on the number of electrons in the outer shell; this is the reason for all the elements in the one group having similar chemical properties,

e.g. all the alkali metals are stored under oil because they are very reactive.

Important numbers

☐ Each element in the Periodic Table has its own **atomic number** ... this gives the number of protons in an atom of an element.

☐ Since atoms are neutral and the charge on an electron is equal and opposite to the charge on a proton, the atomic number also gives the number of electrons in an atom (but not in an ion ... see notes on ionic bonding on page 26).

☐ An element can be defined as a collection of atoms all with the same atomic number (or all with the same number of protons).

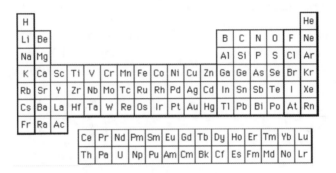

☐ Both the proton and the neutron have a mass of 1 amu; the **mass number** of an atom of an element is the number of protons (atomic number) plus the number of neutrons in the atom.

☐ The atomic number and the mass number provide all the information necessary to calculate the number of protons, neutrons and electrons in an atom.

Atomic number	see Periodic Table
Mass number	not on Periodic Table (has to be given)
Number of protons	equal to atomic number
Number of neutrons	mass number minus atomic number
Number of electrons	equal to number of protons

Example: Calculate the number of protons, neutrons and electrons in an atom of lithium with a mass number of 7.

Atomic number	3
Mass number	7
Number of protons = atomic number	3
Number of neutrons = mass number – atomic number	4
Number of electrons = number of protons	3

> *Note that the mass number of an atom of an element cannot be found in the Data Booklet.*

Nuclide notation

☐ The atomic number and the mass number can be written with the symbol of the element in nuclide notation.

Mass number - 35
Atomic number - 17 Cl

Example: Calculate the number of protons, neutrons and electrons in an atom of oxygen with nuclide notation: $^{18}_{8}O$

Atomic number	8
Mass number	18
Number of protons = atomic number	8
Number of neutrons = mass number – atomic number	10
Number of electrons = number of protons	8

☐ The atomic number is not always given … knowing the element, the atomic number can be found from a Periodic Table.

Isotopes

☐ Atoms of the same element always have the same number of protons (same atomic number).

☐ However, atoms of the same element can be different ... they can have different numbers of neutrons; this means that the mass numbers will not be the same.

☐ Atoms of the same element with different numbers of neutrons are called **isotopes**,

e.g. there are two isotopes of chlorine.

	$^{35}_{17}Cl$	$^{37}_{17}Cl$	
Symbol	Cl	Cl	same
Atomic number	17	17	same
Number of protons	17	17	same
Number of electrons	17	17	same
Mass number	35	37	different
Number of neutrons	18	20	different

☐ Isotopes show similar chemical reactions because the different kinds of atom still have the same number of electrons, i.e. electron arrangement.

Relative atomic mass (atomic weight)

☐ Most elements exist as a mixture of isotopes, each isotope has a different mass number, but for all elements the relative proportion of each isotope is always the same; this allows the atomic mass of an 'average' atom to be calculated.

☐ This mass is called the **relative atomic mass (atomic weight)**.

☐ For some elements the relative atomic mass (atomic weight) is shown on page 4 in the Data Booklet.

☐ The relative proportions of isotopes of different elements are shown below.

^{35}Cl	75%	^{1}H	99.98%
^{37}Cl	25%	^{2}H	0.015%
		^{3}H	Trace
^{12}C	98.89%	^{16}O	99.76%
^{13}C	1.11%	^{17}O	0.037%
^{14}C	Trace	^{18}O	0.204%

☐ The relative atomic mass of each of the elements is not a whole number because it is the mass of an 'average' atom.

☐ Chlorine has a relative atomic mass of 35.5; the average atomic mass is between 35 and 37 and closer to 35 because ^{35}Cl is more abundant than ^{37}Cl.

☐ The relative atomic mass is often listed as a whole number because one of the isotopes is much more abundant than the others and so the average mass is very close to a whole number,

   e.g. hydrogen (relative atomic mass 1), carbon (relative atomic mass 12) and oxygen (relative atomic mass 16).

4   Covalent bonding

Covalent bonds

☐   The join between different atoms in an element or a compound is called a bond.

$$\overset{\displaystyle O}{\underset{\displaystyle H \qquad H}{\diagup \diagdown}}$$

single covalent bonds

☐   One kind of bond is called a **covalent bond**,

e.g. in water, a compound of hydrogen and oxygen, there are two single covalent bonds between hydrogen and oxygen atoms, each represented with a line (—).

☐   A covalent compound is a substance with covalent bonds.

☐   A group of atoms held together by covalent bonds is called a **molecule**; a substance made up of molecules has covalent bonds holding the atoms together.

☐   Covalent bonds form when atoms of non-metal elements join with other atoms of non-metal elements.

☐   Some molecules have more than one covalent bond between the same atoms,

$$O{=}C{=}O$$

double covalent bonds

e.g. in carbon dioxide, a compound of carbon and oxygen, there are two double covalent bonds between carbon and oxygen atoms, each represented with two lines (=).

☐   Some molecules have a triple covalent bond between atoms (≡),

$$H{-}C{\equiv}C{-}H$$

one triple covalent bond; two single covalent bonds

e.g. in ethyne, a compound of carbon and hydrogen, there is a triple covalent bond between the carbon atoms and two single covalent bonds between carbon and hydrogen atoms.

Chemical formulae

☐ The **chemical formula** (or formula) for a covalent substance gives the number of atoms of each element in a molecule; the number of atoms of each element in the molecule is indicated by a subscript after the symbol of the element (the subscript "1" is not written in).

Example 1: water

Each molecule of water has two hydrogen atoms and one oxygen atom so the chemical formula for water is H_2O.

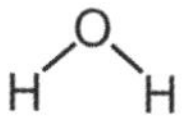

H—O—H
water

Example 2: carbon dioxide

The chemical formula for carbon dioxide is CO_2.

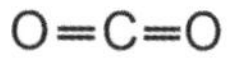

O=C=O
carbon dioxide

Example 3: ethanol

The chemical formula for ethanol is C_2H_6O.

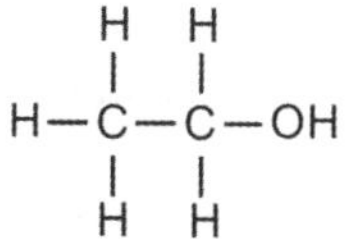

H—C—C—OH
ethanol

Covalent compounds with meaningful names

☐ The formula for some covalent compounds is indicated by the prefix in the second part of the name.

Prefix	Meaning
mono	one
di	two
tri	three
tetra	four
penta	five
hexa	six

e.g. the formula for sulphur trioxide is SO_3.

Covalent bonding: using outer electron shells

☐ The noble gases are unreactive elements; atoms of these elements have filled outer electron shells (energy levels).

☐ Helium has 2 electrons in the first electron shell.

☐ Neon, argon, krypton and xenon have 8 electrons in the outer electron shell.

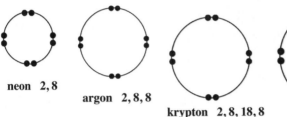

neon   2, 8

argon   2, 8, 8

krypton   2, 8, 18, 8

xenon   2, 8, 18, 18, 8

☐ In a covalent bond there is the sharing of pairs of outer electrons between two non-metal atoms; this enables the atoms that are bonded together to have the same electron arrangement as a noble gas.

☐ Only electrons in the outer energy level (the outside of the atom) are involved in the sharing.

☐ An **electron sharing diagram** can be used to show the sharing of electron pairs that make up covalent bonds; this can also be used to write the chemical formula for a covalent compound.

Example 1:   hydrogen chloride

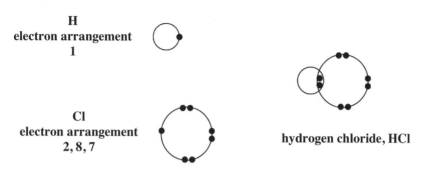

H
electron arrangement
1

Cl
electron arrangement
2, 8, 7

hydrogen chloride, HCl

In the molecule, the hydrogen can be considered to have 2 electrons in the first electron shell; in the molecule, the chlorine atom can be considered to have 8 electrons in the third electron shell.

Example 2:   nitrogen hydride

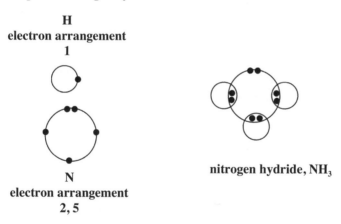

H
electron arrangement
1

N
electron arrangement
2, 5

nitrogen hydride, NH$_3$

In the molecule, the hydrogen can be considered to have 2 electrons in the first electron shell; in the molecule, the nitrogen atom can be considered to have 8 electrons in the second electron shell.

Electron clouds

☐ An **electron cloud** (or orbital) is a region of space in which one or two electrons can be found; a good model of an electron cloud is an inflated balloon without a skin and with no air in it; one (or two) electrons, like flies, can buzz around inside!

☐ Electron clouds have particular shapes depending on the electron shell (energy level).

☐ The electron cloud of the first shell (the one closest to the nucleus) is shaped like a **sphere**.

first shell

☐ The four clouds of the second shell point towards the corners of a **tetrahedron**.

second shell

☐ The third shell is an even larger tetrahedral shape.

third shell

☐ Each cloud can hold one or two electrons.

☐ Electrons fill up electron clouds by entering empty clouds where possible, i.e. pairing in the second and third shells only takes place when all four clouds are half-filled.

Example 1: hydrogen
An atom of hydrogen (atomic number 1) has 1 electron in the first shell. This electron is in a spherical electron cloud.

Example 2: nitrogen
An atom of nitrogen (atomic number 7) has 7 electrons arranged 2, 5.

The electrons in the outer shell are arranged in four clouds that point towards the corners of a tetrahedron.

Covalent bonding: using electron clouds

☐ Atoms in a molecule have the stable electron arrangement of a noble gas; the covalent bonds are formed by the merging of half-filled outer electron clouds so that the electrons are shared in pairs.

☐ When drawing electron-sharing diagrams to show how the outer electron clouds merge to form covalent bonds, the clouds tend to be drawn flattened down.

Example: hydrogen oxide

An atom of oxygen (atomic number 8) has 8 electrons arranged 2, 6.

A drawing of the electrons in the outer shell can be flattened down as shown.

The noble gas nearest to oxygen is neon (atomic number 10) with the 10 electrons arranged 2, 8.

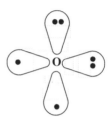

An atom of hydrogen has 1 electron in the first shell.

The noble gas nearest to hydrogen is helium with 2 electrons in the outer shell.

In a molecule of hydrogen oxide, one oxygen atom is joined to two atoms of hydrogen by the merging of half-filled clouds as shown.

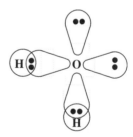

Both atoms in the molecule can be considered to have the stable electron arrangement of a noble gas.

Shapes of molecules

☐ The chemical formula for a covalent substance indicates the number of atoms of each element in the molecule; it does not give any information about the shape of the molecule.

☐ The shapes of molecules are (usually) based on the tetrahedron arrangement of electron clouds.

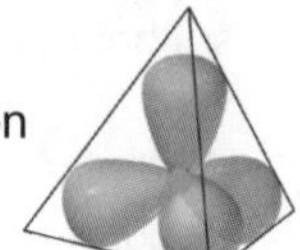

☐ Molecules with two atoms are linear,

    e.g. hydrogen chloride, HCl.   H—Cl

☐ Water is **not** linear because the shape of the molecule is based on the two bonds pointing towards the corners of a tetrahedron; water molecules are two-dimensional (flat).

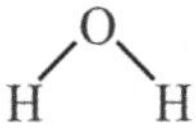

☐ Others are three-dimensional,

    e.g. nitrogen hydride,   *carbon tetrachloride,*

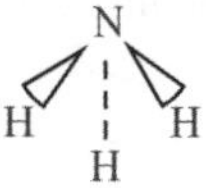

       NH₃   *CCl₄*

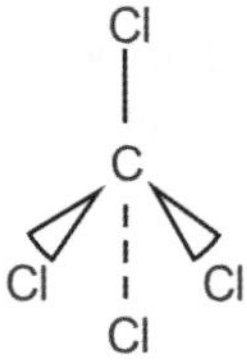

☐ The **full structural formula** shows the shape of a molecule.

☐ When drawing the full structural formula, molecules are drawn flattened down,

    e.g. the full structural formula for carbon tetrachloride is:

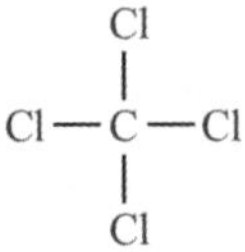

$$Cl-\underset{\underset{Cl}{|}}{\overset{\overset{Cl}{|}}{C}}-Cl$$

Diatomic molecules

☐ Molecules made up of only two atoms are called **diatomic molecules** ('di' meaning two),

   e.g. hydrogen chloride, HCl, (one hydrogen atom and one chlorine atom); carbon monoxide, CO, (one carbon atom and one oxygen atom).

☐ Certain elements normally exist as diatomic molecules; since diatomic molecules contain two atoms, the chemical formula for an element that is made up of diatomic molecules is X_2, where X is the symbol for the element, *e.g. hydrogen is written H_2.*

☐ The seven common elements that exist as diatomic molecules are hydrogen (H_2), oxygen (O_2), nitrogen (N_2), fluorine (F_2), chlorine (Cl_2), bromine (Br_2) and iodine (I_2).

☐ By the sharing of the outer electrons, atoms of these elements can be considered to have the outer electron arrangement of a noble gas.

☐ In five elements, the two atoms in the molecule share one electron pair to form a single covalent bond:

   H—H   F—F   Cl—Cl   Br—Br   I—I

☐ In oxygen, the two atoms in the molecule share two pairs of electrons to form a double covalent bond: O=O

☐ In nitrogen, the two atoms in the molecule share three pairs of electrons to form a triple covalent bond: N≡N

☐ We have to think in terms of the three-dimensional arrangement of electron clouds in nitrogen to appreciate why the two atoms in the diatomic molecule can form a triple covalent bond.

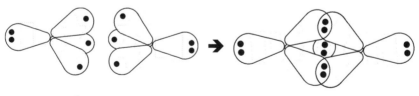

nitrogen atoms   **nitrogen molecule**

Writing formulae for covalent compounds

□ Covalent compounds are (usually) made up of atoms of non-metal elements.

□ The formula for covalent compounds can be found by drawing electron sharing diagrams.

□ The following is a quick way to find the formula for a covalent compound; it is based on the number of bonds that an atom forms; this is equal to the number of 'extra' electrons that an atom requires to reach the same electron arrangement as a noble gas.

	Group 4	Group 5	Group 6	Group 7
Number of outer electrons	4	5	6	7
Number of 'extra' electrons needed	4	3	2	1
Number of bonds formed	4	3	2	1

□ An atom of hydrogen is 1 electron short of an atom of helium so hydrogen forms 1 bond.

Example: carbon fluoride

Step 1: Use the Periodic Table to write symbols for the elements.

$$C \qquad\qquad F$$

Step 2: Use the Periodic Table to put in the number of bonds that will be formed by each atom.

$$-\overset{\displaystyle |}{\underset{\displaystyle |}{C}}- \qquad\qquad -F$$

Step 3: Complete the bonding picture.

$$F-\overset{\displaystyle F}{\underset{\displaystyle F}{C}}-F$$

Step 4: Write the formula CF_4

Energy considerations

☐ The protons give a positive charge to the nucleus of the atom; the electrons give a negative charge to the part of the atom surrounding the nucleus.

☐ In a covalent bond the sharing of electron pairs (merging of half-filled clouds) increases the negative charge in the overlap region.

☐ The forces of attraction between the positive nuclei of both atoms and the electrons in the overlap region holds the atoms together,

e.g. hydrogen

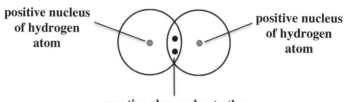

positive nucleus of hydrogen atom

positive nucleus of hydrogen atom

negative charge due to the electrons in the overlap region

+ve ⟷ -ve ⟷ +ve

☐ A covalent bond is the attraction of two positive nuclei for a shared pair of electrons.

☐ A lot of energy is required to overcome the forces of attraction, i.e. to break covalent bonds … so covalent bonds are strong.

5 Ionic bonding

Ionic compounds

☐ Some elements and compounds are made up of molecules; there is covalent bonding in these substances; all the atoms are atoms of non-metal elements.

☐ Other compounds are made of charged particles called **ions**; these compounds are called **ionic compounds**.

☐ Ionic compounds contain both metal ions (positively charged) and non-metal ions (negatively charged).

☐ Positive ions attract negative ions; the forces of attraction across the oppositely charged ions are known as **ionic bonds** and keep the ions locked together.

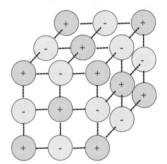

☐ The arrangement of ions in a solid is called a **crystal lattice**; this arrangement goes on and on in all directions, i.e. the arrangement is three-dimensional.

Formation of ions

☐ In covalent bonding, atoms share electrons to reach the same stable electron arrangement as an atom of a noble gas; the formation of ions by losing or gaining electrons is another way in which atoms can reach a stable electron arrangement.

☐ Metal ions have a **positive charge** (+).

Example 1: The sodium ion

The atomic number of sodium is 11. The electron arrangement is 2, 8, 1.

Looking at the atomic numbers, the nearest noble gas to sodium is neon with electron arrangement 2, 8.
A sodium atom can reach this electron arrangement by losing one electron. Since an electron has one unit of negative charge, the charge left on the sodium ion will be one-positive.

The sodium ion is represented Na⁺ (there is no need to include the '1' before the +).

sodium atom
Na
2, 8, 1

sodium ion
Na⁺
2, 8

Example 2: The calcium ion

The atomic number of calcium is 20. The electron arrangement is 2, 8, 8, 2.

Looking at the atomic numbers, the nearest noble gas to calcium is argon with electron arrangement 2, 8, 8.
A calcium atom can reach this electron arrangement by losing two electrons. Since an electron has one unit of negative charge, the charge left on the calcium ion will be two-positive.

The calcium ion is represented Ca^{2+}.

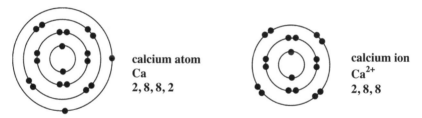

calcium atom
Ca
2, 8, 8, 2

calcium ion
Ca^{2+}
2, 8, 8

☐ Non-metal ions have a **negative charge** (-).

Example 3: The chloride ion

The atomic number of chlorine is 17. The electron arrangement is 2, 8, 7.

Looking at the atomic numbers, the nearest noble gas to chlorine is argon with electron arrangement 2, 8, 8.
A chlorine atom can reach this electron arrangement by gaining one electron. Since an electron has one unit of negative charge, the charge on the chloride ion will be one-negative.

The chloride ion is represented Cl⁻ (again, there is no need to include the '1' before the -).

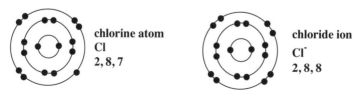

chlorine atom
Cl
2, 8, 7

chloride ion
Cl⁻
2, 8, 8

Example 4:   The oxide ion

The atomic number of oxygen is 8. The electron arrangement is 2, 6.

Looking at the atomic numbers, the nearest noble gas to oxygen is neon with electron arrangement 2, 8.
An oxygen atom can reach this electron arrangement by gaining two electrons. Since an electron has one unit of negative charge, the charge on the oxide ion will be two-negative.

The oxide ion is represented O^{2-}.

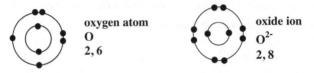

☐   A quick way to find the charge on an ion is to look in the Data Booklet for the group in the Periodic Table that the element is in.

☐   The charge on a metal ion is the same as the group that the element is in; this is the same as the number of electrons that would need to be lost to form the stable electron arrangement of a noble gas.

☐   The charge on a non-metal ion is found by subtracting the group number from 8; this is the same as the number of electrons that would need to be gained to form the stable electron arrangement of a noble gas.

Group 1	Group 2	Group 3	Group 4	Group 5	Group 6	Group 7
1+	2+	3+		3-	2-	1-

☐   It is easier for atoms of elements in Groups 1 to 3 to lose electrons to reach noble gas electron arrangements; this helps to explain why atoms of metal elements do **not** form covalent bonds.

Nuclide notation: ions

☐ The atomic number and the mass number can be written with the symbol of the element.

$$\text{Mass number - 23} \atop \text{Atomic number - 11} \quad \text{Na}^+$$

☐ The atomic number gives the number of protons in the ion; this is not always given … knowing the symbol for the element, the atomic number can be found from a Periodic Table.

☐ The charge on the ion allows the number of electrons to be found; positive ions have more protons than electrons: negative ions have more electrons than protons.

☐ The mass number gives the number of protons plus the number of neutrons in the ion.

Example 1: Calculate the number of protons, neutrons and electrons in an atom of magnesium with nuclide notation: $^{26}_{12}\text{Mg}^{2+}$

Atomic number	12
Mass number	26
Number of protons = atomic number	12
Number of neutrons = mass number – atomic number	14
Number of electrons = number of protons - charge	10

Example 2: Calculate the number of protons, neutrons and electrons in an atom of sulphur with nuclide notation: $^{32}\text{S}^{2-}$

Atomic number (from Periodic Table)	16
Mass number	32
Number of protons = atomic number	16
Number of neutrons = mass number – atomic number	16
Number of electrons = number of protons + charge	18

The significance of the formula

☐ Since small molecules consist of definite number of atoms held together by covalent bonds, the chemical formula for a covalent compound shows the actual number of atoms in each molecule,

e.g. *H_2O shows **two** hydrogen atoms joined with **one** oxygen atom;*

*$C_6H_{12}O_6$ shows **six** carbon atoms, **twelve** hydrogen atoms and **six** oxygen atoms in a molecule.*

covalent compounds

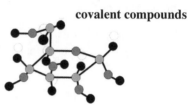

☐ On the other hand, because a large number of positive and negative ions are held together by ionic bonds to form a crystal lattice, the chemical formula for an ionic compound only indicates the relative number of ions present,

e.g. *NaCl shows **equal** numbers Na^+ and Cl^- ions;*

*K_2S shows **twice** as many K^+ ions as S^{2-} ions;*

*MgF_2 shows **twice** as many F^- ions as Mg^{2+} ions.*

ionic compound

Writing formulae for ionic compounds: using electron arrangements

☐ Ions have the same electron arrangement as atoms of a noble gas; this is achieved by the transfer of electrons from metal atoms to non-metal atoms.

☐ Since electrons have a negative charge, metal atoms will be left with a positive charge and non-metal atoms will have gained a negative charge.

Example 1: lithium chloride

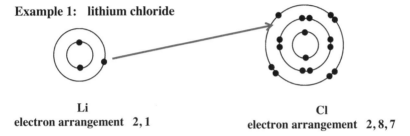

Li	**Cl**
electron arrangement 2, 1	electron arrangement 2, 8, 7

The loss of one electron from the lithium atom to the chlorine atom gives the lithium ion the stable electron arrangement of a helium atom and the chloride ion the stable electron arrangement of an argon atom.
The formula for lithium chloride is **LiCl**.

Example 2: magnesium fluoride

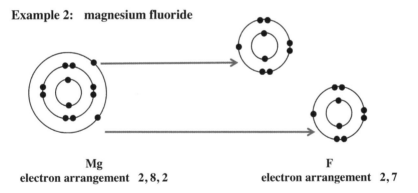

Mg	**F**
electron arrangement 2, 8, 2	electron arrangement 2, 7

The loss of one electron from the magnesium atom to the fluorine atom gives the fluoride ion the stable electron arrangement of a neon atom. However, two fluorine atoms are required for the magnesium atom to lose two electrons and reach the stable electron arrangement of a neon atom.
The formula for magnesium fluoride is **MgF$_2$**.

Writing formulae for ionic compounds: balancing charge

☐ The charge on many ions can be worked out from the electron arrangements on page 1 of the Data Booklet.

Group 1	Group 2	Group 3	Group 4	Group 5	Group 6	Group 7
1+	2+	3+		3-	2-	1-

☐ In an ionic compound, the charge on all positive ions must balance the charge on all negative ions.

☐ Since the overall charge is neutral, the formula for an ionic compound can be worked out by finding the relative number of each ion required to make the overall charge zero.

☐ The **ionic formula** shows the charges on the ions.

Example 1: sodium chloride

	positive ion	negative ion
	Na^+	Cl^-

ionic formula $Na^+ Cl^-$

formula   **NaCl**

Example 2: potassium oxide

	positive ion	negative ion
	K^+	O^{2-}

ionic formula $(K^+)_2 O^{2-}$

formula   **K_2O**

Writing formulae for ionic compounds: metals that have variable charge

☐ Some metals have ions with more than one charge; in compounds of these metals the charge is shown in Roman numerals after the name of the metal element,

e.g. in copper(I) oxide the charge of the copper is one-positive (Cu^+);
in iron(II) chloride the charge of the iron is two-positive (Fe^{2+})

Example 1:   copper(I) oxide

	positive ion	negative ion
	Cu^+	O^{2-}
ionic formula	$(Cu^+)_2O^{2-}$	
formula	**Cu_2O**	

Example 2:   iron(II) chloride

	positive ion	negative ion
	Fe^{2+}	Cl^-
ionic formula	$Fe^{2+}(Cl^-)_2$	
formula	**$FeCl_2$**	

Writing formulae for ionic compounds: compounds with group ions

☐ A number of ions consist of a group of atoms that tend to stay together during reactions; these are called **group ions**.

☐ The charge is on the whole group and not on any particular atom,

e.g. the sulphate ion

formula for the ion $\left(SO_4^{2-}\right)$ **the charge on the ion is 2-negative**

□ The formula for and charge of a group ion can be found on page 4 of the Data Booklet.

□ The presence of a group ion can usually be recognised from the -ate or -ite name ending that indicates the presence of oxygen; the exceptions are the ammonium ion and the hydroxide ion.

□ Apart from the ammonium ion, which has a positive charge like the metal ions, all the group ions have a negative charge.

Example 1: sodium nitrate

	positive ion	negative ion
	Na^+	(NO_3^-)
ionic formula	$Na^+(NO_3^-)$ or $Na^+NO_3^-$	
formula	$NaNO_3$	

> *Always begin by putting the formula for the group ion in brackets. When the subscript number for the group would be 1, as above, the brackets can be removed. When the subscript number for the group is greater than 1, brackets are essential.*

Example 2: calcium nitrate

	positive ion	negative ion
	Ca^{2+}	(NO_3^-)
ionic formula	$Ca^{2+}(NO_3^-)_2$	
formula	$Ca(NO_3)_2$	

The ionic formula for calcium nitrate is $Ca^{2+}(NO_3^-)_2$ not $Ca^{2+}NO_3{^-}_2$.
The formula has one calcium ion for every two nitrate ions. This gives a total of one calcium atom, two nitrogen atoms and six oxygen atoms.

6 Properties of substances

Conduction of electricity

☐ Electricity is a flow of charged particles; what happens when a substance is included as part of an electrical circuit gives information about the particles in the substance and the way they are held together.

☐ The terminals through which the electrical current enters and leaves the substance under test are called the **electrodes**; these are usually made of graphite, a form of carbon that conducts electricity but is comparatively unreactive.

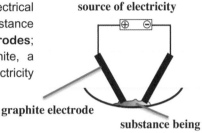

source of electricity

graphite electrode

substance being tested

☐ Elements and compounds that conduct electricity are **conductors**; elements and compounds that do **not** conduct electricity are **non-conductors**.

Elements: conductors or non-conductors?

☐ The elements in the Periodic Table can be divided into metals and non-metals.

☐ Some non-metal elements are made up of atoms; others are made up of molecules, i.e. atoms held together by covalent bonds.

☐ All metal elements conduct electricity both as solids and liquids (think about mercury).

☐ All non-metal elements (except for one) do **not** conduct electricity; carbon (in the form of graphite) is the exception (think about the use as electrodes).

☐ Atoms are made up of a nucleus that contains positive particles; negative particles called electrons move around outside the nucleus.

outer electrons

☐ In metals, the outer electrons are loosely held; the flow of electricity in metals is a flow of the loosely held electrons in a definite direction.

Covalent compounds: conductors or non-conductors?

☐ Most covalent compounds are made up of molecules (see note on covalent network structures on page 42).

☐ Covalent molecular compounds are similar to elements that are made up of molecules ... they do **not** conduct electricity when solid, when liquid nor when in solution.

☐ Elements and compounds that are made up of molecules do **not** conduct electricity because molecules do not have an overall charge.

Ionic compounds: conductors or non-conductors?

☐ Compounds that contain both a metal and a non-metal element are (usually) ionic compounds.

☐ Ionic compounds are made up of charged particles called ions; in the solid, the forces of attraction keep the ions locked together.

☐ Ionic compounds do **not** conduct electricity when solid since the ions in a solid are unable to move.

☐ Ionic compounds do conduct electricity when In a solution, since the ions in the dissolved solid become free to move.

☐ Ionic compounds also conduct electricity when molten (liquid at a temperature above the melting point), since the ions in the molten compound also become free to move.

Making use of electricity

☐ Electrons flow through metal wires; with an alternating current (a.c.) supply, the direction of the movement of the electrons is always changing; with a direct current (d.c.) supply, the direction of the movement of electrons is always the same.

☐ Ionic compounds conduct as a solution and also when molten (liquid state); the ions are free to move.

☐ The passage of electricity through a solution of an ionic compound results in the movement of ions to the electrodes; the chemical reactions taking place at the electrodes cause the solution to break up; this process is called **electrolysis**; the solution between the electrodes that does the conducting is called the **electrolyte**.

☐ The passage of electricity through a molten ionic compound is also known as **electrolysis**; the chemical reactions taking place at the electrodes cause the molten compound to break up.

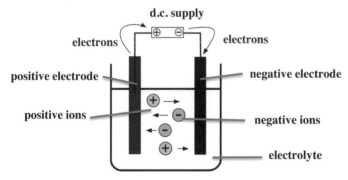

☐ In order to keep the ions moving in the one direction, a d.c. supply is always used for electrolysis.

☐ The electrode that is connected to the positive terminal of the supply is 'positive' (sometimes labelled +ve or +); the other is 'negative' (sometimes labelled -ve or -); the electrodes attract oppositely charged ions during electrolysis.

☐ At the negative electrode, positive ions gain electrons to form atoms; at the positive electrode, negative ions lose electrons to form atoms.

☐ The electrodes are usually made of carbon (in the form of graphite), an element that conducts electricity but is comparatively unreactive.

Electrolysis of copper(II) chloride solution

☐ The electrolysis of copper(II) chloride solution causes the solution to break up as the ions separate out and chemical reactions take place at each of the electrodes.

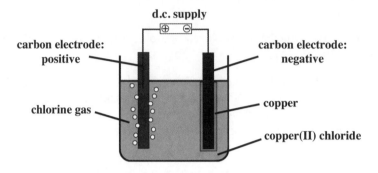

☐ At the negative electrode, copper is formed; the positive copper ions gain electrons to form copper atoms.
The reaction taking place is:

$$Cu^{2+} (aq) \quad + \quad 2e^- \quad \longrightarrow \quad Cu (s)$$

☐ At the positive electrode, chlorine is formed; the negative chloride ions lose electrons to form atoms (and then molecules).
The reaction taking place is:

$$2Cl^- (aq) \quad \longrightarrow \quad Cl_2 (g) \quad + \quad 2e^-$$

Electrolysis of molten lead iodide (liquid)

- The molten lead iodide breaks up as the ions separate out and new products are formed by the chemical reaction at each of the electrodes.

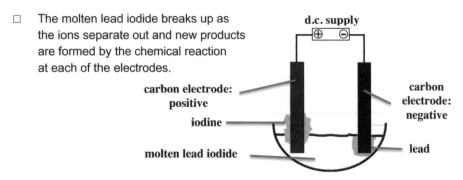

d.c. supply

carbon electrode: positive

iodine

molten lead iodide

carbon electrode: negative

lead

- At the negative electrode, lead is formed; positive lead ions gain electrons to form atoms.
  The reaction taking place is:

$$Pb^{2+} (l) \quad + \quad 2e^- \quad \longrightarrow \quad Pb (s)$$

- At the positive electrode, iodine is formed; the negative iodide ions lose electrons to form atoms (and then molecules).
  The reaction taking place is:

$$2I^- (l) \quad \longrightarrow \quad I_2 (g) + 2e^-$$

Colours of compounds

- Many ionic compounds are white; the ions are colourless and they dissolve in water to form colourless solutions,

  e.g. sodium chloride is white since the Na^+ and Cl^- ions are colourless.

- Some ionic compounds are coloured; one of the ions has to be coloured and the compounds dissolve in water to form coloured solutions,

  e.g. copper(II) sulphate is blue since the Cu^{2+} ion is blue and the SO_4^{2-} ion is colourless.

- For an ionic compound $X^+ Y^-$, the colour of the compound is determined by the colour of X^+ and Y^-.

- Ions are not usually the same colour as atoms of the element.

  e.g. copper ions are blue but copper atoms are brown;
  bromide ions are colourless but bromine molecules are brown.

Electrolysis of copper chromate solution

☐ Copper ions are positive and blue in colour; chromate ions are negative and yellow in colour.

☐ The colour of copper chromate solution is green, a 'blend' of the colour of the copper and chromate ions of the compound.

☐ A yellow colour is seen at the positive electrode; the negative chromate ions are attracted to this electrode.

☐ A blue colour is seen at the negative electrode; the positive copper ions are attracted to this electrode.

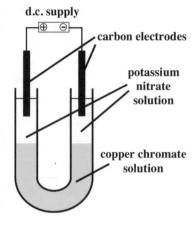

☐ Potassium nitrate solution is a colourless solution; the solution contains ions that can move to complete the circuit.

Solids, liquids and gases

☐ The state of a compound at room temperature is an indication of the type of bonding in the compound.

State at room temperature	Type of bonding
Solid	all ionic a few covalent
Liquid	covalent
Gas	covalent

☐ All ionic compounds are solid at room temperature.

☐ The bonding in compounds that are solid at room temperature could be covalent or ionic.

☐ Compounds that are liquid or gas at room temperature have covalent bonding.

Differences in bonding and structure

(a) Ionic compounds

□ Ions in a crystal lattice are held together by strong forces of attraction across the oppositely charged ions in the crystal lattice; a lot of energy is needed to separate the ions.

sodium chloride

□ This is the reason that ionic compounds are all solid at room temperature, i.e. melting and boiling points are well above room temperature,

e.g. sodium chloride has a melting point of 801°C.

(b) Covalent molecular substances

□ When a covalent molecular substance melts or boils, the heat energy makes the molecules move faster and further apart.

□ The forces of attraction holding together the different atoms in a covalent bond are strong and so a lot of energy is required to break the covalent bonds.

□ However, the forces of attraction holding different molecules together are weaker than covalent bonds and so less energy is required to separate the molecules.

□ This is the reason covalent molecular substances are liquids or gases at room temperature.

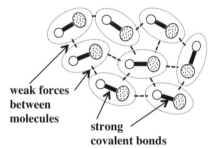

weak forces between molecules

strong covalent bonds

□ As molecular mass increases, the strength of the forces of attraction between different molecules increases; as a result, the energy required to separate the molecules increases and covalent molecular substances with a high mass can be solid at room temperature,

e.g. going down Group 7 of the Periodic Table, fluorine and chlorine are gases, bromine is a liquid and iodine is a solid at room temperature; as the number of carbon atoms in the alkanes increases, the boiling point increases (see notes on alkanes on page 83).

(c) Covalent network substances

- [ ] Some covalent substances do **not** exist as molecules ... a very large number of atoms are joined by covalent bonds to form a giant network structure.

- [ ] Unlike covalent molecular substances, covalent network substances are **not** made up of a definite number of atoms.

- [ ] Covalent bonds, like the forces of attraction between ions, are strong; a lot of energy is needed to break the covalent bonds and separate the atoms; this is the reason that covalent network substances are all solid at room temperature.

- [ ] **Diamond** is a covalent network element made up of carbon atoms; each atom is surrounded by four other carbon atoms at the corners of a tetrahedron.

- [ ] Covalent compounds can also exist as network structures,

  e.g. silicon dioxide.

diamond

Solubility

- [ ] A **solvent** is a liquid in which substances can dissolve; it is often useful to know whether or not a substance is soluble or insoluble in a particular solvent.

- [ ] The most common solvent is water; solids, liquids and gases can all dissolve in water to form an **aqueous solution**,

  e.g. salt (a solid), alcohol (a liquid) and carbon dioxide (a gas) all dissolve in water.

- [ ] Compounds that are soluble in water are likely to have ionic bonding,

  e.g. salt (sodium chloride).

- [ ] Solvents other than water are **non-aqueous** solvents; the bonding in these solvents is covalent.

- [ ] Compounds that are soluble in non-aqueous solvents are likely to have covalent bonding,

  e.g. nail polish is insoluble in water but can be removed by dissolving in acetone; stains caused by paints made from covalent substances cannot be removed by water ... white spirit is used.

☐ As a rough guide:
* many ionic compounds dissolve in water but **not** in non-aqueous solvents;
* most covalent compounds dissolve in non-aqueous solvents but **not** in water.

☐ There are exceptions to the above,

e.g. sugar, $C_{12}H_{22}O_{11}$, is a covalent compound and is soluble in water.

7 Chemical equations

Writing formulae: using combining powers (valency method)

☐ The chemical formula for a compound can always be worked out by considering the bonding; there is, however, a shorter method that uses the **combining powers** (**valencies**) of the elements involved; this method works for both covalent and ionic compounds.

☐ Valency is a number that gives the combining power of an element; it can be found from the element's group in the Periodic Table.

Group 1	Group 2	Group 3	Group 4	Group 5	Group 6	Group 7
1	2	3	4	3	2	1

☐ For metals that show variable charge the combining power corresponds to the charge on the ion,

e.g. in iron(II) oxide the combining power of the iron ion is 2;

in copper(I) oxide the combining power of the copper ion is 1.

☐ For group ions, the combining power corresponds to the charge on the ion,

e.g. in SO_4^{2-} the combining power of the ion is 2;

in NO_3^- the combining power of the ion is 1.

Example 1: hydrogen sulphide

Step 1	Write atoms with combining powers in this form	1 2 H S
Step 2	Exchange the combining powers	1 ⤬ 2 H S
Step 3	Ignore the number 1 to give the chemical formula	H_2S

Example 2: potassium sulphate

Step 1	Write atoms and group ion (in brackets) with combining powers	1 2 K (SO_4)
Step 2	Exchange combining powers	1 ⤬ 2 K (SO_4)
Step 3	Ignore the number 1 to give the chemical formula	$K_2(SO_4)$ or K_2SO_4

> *The brackets can be removed when the number that is crossed over is 1.*

Example 3:   iron(II) nitrate

Step 1	Write atom and group ion (in brackets) with combining powers	2 1 Fe (NO_3)
Step 2	Exchange combining powers	2 ⤬ 1 Fe (NO_3)
Step 3	Ignore the number 1 to give the chemical formula	$Fe(NO_3)_2$

An extra step is sometimes necessary when the combining powers can be cancelled, e.g. 4 and 2 (becoming 2 and 1), 2 and 2 (becoming 1 and 1).

Example 4:   silicon oxide

Step 1	Write atoms with combining powers	4 2 Si O
Step 2	Cancel the numbers 4 and 2 to give 2 and 1	2 1 Si O
Step 3	Exchange combining powers	2 ⤬ 1 Si O
Step 4	Ignore the number 1 to give the chemical formula	SiO_2

State symbols

☐ Suffixes can be used after the formula to show the chemical state of the substances.

Suffix	Meaning	Example
(s)	solid	Cu (s)
(l)	liquid	H_2O (l)
(g)	gas	O_2 (g)
(aq)	dissolved in water	$NaCl$ (aq)

Word equations

☐ In a chemical reaction, substances present at the start change to make new substances.

☐ The starting substances in chemical reactions are called the **reactants**; the new substances which are produced are called the **products**.

☐ The chemical reaction can be written in a short-hand form, called a **word equation**.

☐ In a word equation:
* the '+' sign means 'and';
* the ' ⟶ ' sign means 'changed into';
* the reactants come in front of the arrow;
* the products come after the arrow.

Example 1: The food in our bodies reacts with oxygen taken from the air to produce water and carbon dioxide which we breathe out.

The word equation is:

food   +   oxygen ⟶ water   +   carbon dioxide
      the reactants   the products

Example 2: When silver oxide is heated, the compound breaks up to give silver and oxygen.

The word equation is:

silver oxide   ⟶   silver   +   oxygen

Example 3: In the Haber Process, nitrogen combines with hydrogen at high pressure and a moderately high temperature to produce ammonia.

The word equation is:

nitrogen   +   hydrogen ⟶ ammonia

Equations using formulae

☐ An equation using formulae gives more information than a word equation; it shows the elements involved and the way in which they are joined up in the reactant(s) and product(s).

☐ In a reaction the atoms (or ions) that take part (either as an element or as part of a compound) also make up what is formed.

Example: **burning of hydrogen**
The word equation is:

hydrogen   +   oxygen   ⟶   water

This equation can be written using the formula for each reactant and product:

$$H_2 \quad + \quad O_2 \quad \longrightarrow \quad H_2O$$

☐ The following flow diagram can be used when writing equations; it should be followed for each substance in the equation in turn.

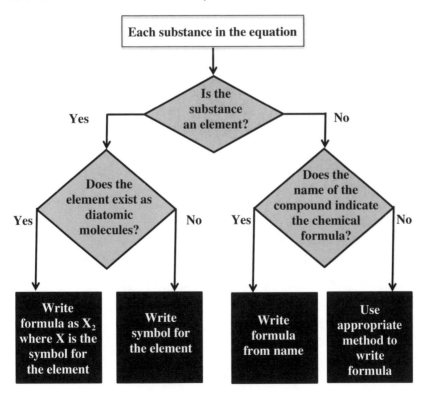

Balanced chemical equations

☐ In a chemical reaction, matter is not created nor destroyed; the number of atoms (or ions) on the reactant side must be equal to the number of atoms (or ions) on the product side.

Example: burning of hydrogen
The unbalanced chemical equation for the burning of hydrogen is:

$$H_2 \quad + \quad O_2 \quad \longrightarrow \quad H_2O$$

However, O_2 has two oxygen atoms in a molecule and the number of oxygens on the product side must equal the number of oxygens on the reactant side. Another H_2O unit is required.

$$H_2 \quad + \quad O_2 \quad \longrightarrow \quad \begin{matrix} H_2O \\ H_2O \end{matrix}$$

Balancing the oxygen gives:

$$H_2 \quad + \quad O_2 \quad \longrightarrow \quad 2H_2O$$

Now four hydrogens are required on the reactant side.

$$\begin{matrix} H_2 \\ H_2 \end{matrix} \quad + \quad O_2 \quad \longrightarrow \quad 2H_2O$$

The balanced chemical equation for the burning of hydrogen is:

$$2H_2 \quad + \quad O_2 \quad \longrightarrow \quad 2H_2O$$

☐ Never change a formula to make an equation balance; equations can only be balanced by putting a number in front of formulae,

e.g. $2H_2$ or $2H_2O$, not H_{22} or H_2O_2;
the formula for water is always H_2O (H_2O_2 is a quite different compound).

Balanced chemical equations

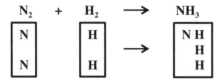

Two nitrogens are required on the product side.
This has to come as NH_3 unit.

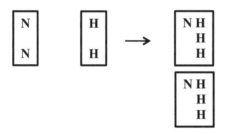

Six hydrogens are required on the reactant side.
These have to come as H_2 units.

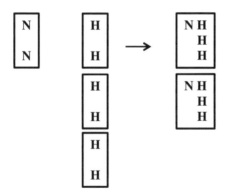

The balanced equation is:

$$N_2 \quad + \quad 3H_2 \quad \longrightarrow \quad 2NH_3$$

8 Chemical calculations

Formula mass

☐ The mass of an atom is measured on the relative atomic mass scale.

☐ The mass of a 'unit' of a compound is called the formula mass.

☐ The formula mass is obtained from the formula by adding together all the relative atomic masses of the atoms (or ions).

☐ The formula mass has no units since atomic masses are measured on a relative scale.

Example 1:   Calculate the formula mass of nitrogen hydride, NH_3

Step 1	Formula		NH_3		
Step 2	Find the relative atomic masses	N 14	H 1		Use the Data Booklet
Step 3	Multiply by the number of atoms	14 x 1	1 x 3		check with formula
Step 4	Do the sum	14	3		calculator?
Step 5	The answer		**17**		check it!

Example 2:   Calculate the formula mass of sodium carbonate, Na_2CO_3

Step 1	Formula		Na_2CO_3	
Step 2	Find the relative atomic masses	Na 23	C 12	O 16
Step 3	Multiply by the number of atoms	23 x 2	12 x 1	16 x 3
Step 4	Do the sum	46 +	12 +	48
Step 5	The answer		**106**	

Example 3:   Calculate the formula mass of calcium hydroxide, $Ca(OH)_2$

Step 1   Formula $Ca(OH)_2$

Step 2   Find the relative atomic masses   Ca   O   H
                                                                    40   16   1

Step 3   Multiply by the number   40   16 x 2   1 x 2
          of atoms

Note that the brackets mean that the 2 refers to both the oxygen and hydrogen.

Step 4   Do the sum   40   +   32   +   2

Step 5   The answer   **74**

The mole

☐ One **mole** of any substance is defined as the formula mass in grams, i.e. the gram formula mass (GFM).

☐ The formula mass of any substance is first calculated from the formula.

☐ To calculate the mass of one mole of the substance, simply change the units to grams.

Example 1:   Calculate the mass of one mole of sodium.

Step 1	Formula	Na
Step 2	Find the relative atomic mass	23
Step 3	Change units to grams	**23 g**

Example 2:   Calculate the mass of one mole of potassium sulphate.

Step 1	Formula		K_2SO_4	
Step 2	Find the relative atomic masses	K 39	S 32	O 16
Step 3	Multiply by the number of atoms	39 x 2	32 x 1	16 x 4
Step 4	Do the sum	78 +	32 +	64
Step 5	Formula mass		174	
Step 6	Change units to grams		**174 g**	

Example 3:   Calculate the mass of two moles of sodium chloride.

Step 1   Formula   NaCl

Step 2   Find the relative atomic masses   Na   Cl
                                                  23   35.5

Step 3   Multiply by the number   23 x 1   35.5 x 1
          of atoms

Step 4   Do the sum   23   +   35.5

Step 5   Formula mass   58.5

Step 6   Change units to grams (GFM)   58.5 g

Step 7   Complete calculation   mass   =   no. of moles x GFM

$$\boxed{m = n \text{ x GFM}}$$ =   2 x 58.5

                                          =   **117 g**

Example 4:   Calculate the number of moles in 36 g of water, H_2O.

Step 1   Formula H_2O

Step 2   Find the relative atomic masses   H   O
                                                  1   16

Step 3   Multiply by the number   1 x 2   16 x 1
          of atoms

Step 4   Do the sum   2   +   16

Step 5   Formula mass   18

Step 6   Change units to grams (GFM)   18 g

Step 7   Complete calculation   no. of moles = $\dfrac{\text{mass}}{\text{GFM}}$

$$\boxed{n = \dfrac{m}{\text{GFM}}}$$ = $\dfrac{36}{18}$

                                          =   **2 mol**

Using concentration

☐ The concentration of an aqueous solution is expressed as the mass of substance dissolved in a certain volume of water.

☐ The concentration can be expressed as grams per litre, g l^{-1}; this can also be written as g/l.

☐ The concentration is often expressed in terms of the number of moles of substance dissolved in water to make 1 litre of solution, i.e. mol l^{-1} (or mol/l).

☐ A solution labelled 1 mol l^{-1} contains **one** mole of substance dissolved in water and made up to one litre of solution; a solution labelled 2 mol l^{-1} contains **two** moles of substance dissolved in water and made up to one litre of solution.

Example 1: **Calculate the number of moles of sodium hydroxide in 100 cm^3 solution, concentration 0.4 mol l^{-1}.**

$$n = CV$$

no. of moles	=	conc x litres
	=	0.4 x 0.1
	=	**0.04 mol**

Example 2: **Calculate the concentration of a solution of hydrochloric acid containing 0.1 mol in 50 cm^3.**

$$C = \frac{n}{V}$$

conc	=	$\dfrac{\text{no. of moles}}{\text{litres}}$
	=	$\dfrac{0.1}{0.05}$
	=	**2 mol l^{-1}**

Example 3: **Calculate the volume of a sodium carbonate solution, concentration 2 mol l^{-1}, that contains 0.5 mol.**

$$V = \frac{n}{C}$$

litres	=	$\dfrac{\text{no. of moles}}{\text{conc}}$
	=	$\dfrac{0.5}{2}$
	=	**0.25 l (250 cm^3)**

Example 4: Calculate the concentration of a solution containing 2 g sodium hydroxide in 50 cm^3 solution.

Step 1   Formula   NaOH

Step 2   Mass of one mole (GFM) $23 + 16 + 1$ = 40 g

Step 3   Number of moles   no. of moles $= \dfrac{mass}{GFM}$

$$\boxed{n = \dfrac{m}{GFM}}$$

$$= \dfrac{2}{40}$$

$$= 0.05 \text{ mol}$$

Step 4   Complete calculation   conc $= \dfrac{\text{no. of moles}}{\text{litres}}$

$$\boxed{C = \dfrac{n}{V}}$$

$$= \dfrac{0.05}{0.05}$$

$$= \mathbf{1 \text{ mol } l^{-1}}$$

Example 5: Calculate the mass of calcium chloride in 25 cm^3 of a solution, concentration 0.1 mol l^{-1}.

Step 1   Number of moles   no. of moles $=$ conc x litres

$$\boxed{n = C \times V}$$

$$= 0.1 \times 0.025$$

$$= 0.0025$$

Step 2   Formula $CaCl_2$

Step 3   Mass of one mole (GFM) $40 + (2 \times 35.5)$ = 111 g

Step 4   Complete calculation   mass $=$ no. of moles x GFM

$$\boxed{m = n \times GFM}$$

$$= 0.0025 \times 111$$

$$= \mathbf{0.2775 \text{ g}}$$

9 Acids and bases

Acids and alkalis

- Acids are commonly found in the lab,

    e.g. hydrochloric acid, sulphuric acid and nitric acid.

- Bottles of acid are labelled with the warning symbol for 'irritant'; any spills must be washed off with water; if you do not do this, your skin will soon feel itchy.

- We often say that an acid 'burns' the skin but this is not the same as what happens when a fuel burns!

- Alkalis are also found in the lab,

    e.g. sodium hydroxide solution.

- Like acids, the bottles are labelled with the warning symbol for 'irritant'; alkalis feel soapy if spilled on your skin; similarly to acids, alkalis 'burn' the skin.

- Acids are all around us in many 'things' that we take for granted,

    e.g. citric acid is found in fruits like oranges and lemons, ethanoic acid in vinegar, hydrochloric acid in the stomach, sulphuric acid in car batteries.

- The same applies to alkalis,

    e.g. they are in oven cleaners, indigestion tablets and toothpaste.

Testing for acids and alkalis

- It would be easy to recognise acids by their sour taste … but this would not be a sensible test for acids!

- Special chemical solutions called indicators can be added to substances to check for acids and alkalis; the most common indicator for acids and alkalis is **Universal indicator** (sometimes called pH indicator).

- Water is said to be neutral … it is neither acid nor alkali.

- Universal indicator is a solution of chemical compounds that in water have a green colour.

- The indicator changes to yellow / orange / red colours in the presence of acids and dark green / blue colours in alkalis but remains green in neutral solutions.

- Universal indicator can be stained on to paper and dried; this makes **pH paper** that can also be used to test for acids and alkalis.

The pH scale

☐ Universal indicator and pH paper can also be used to 'measure' how much acid or alkali is in a solution.

☐ The scale that is used is called the **pH scale**; this is a continuous number scale that runs from below 0 (acid) to above 14 (alkali) with water and neutral solutions having a pH of 7.

☐ Acidity and alkalinity increase as the pH moves away from 7, i.e. the lower the pH of a solution (below 7), the greater the acidity and the higher the pH of a solution (above 7), the greater the alkalinity.

☐ The indicator turns a different colour at each pH number and so the pH of acids and alkalis can be found by colour-matching with a chart.

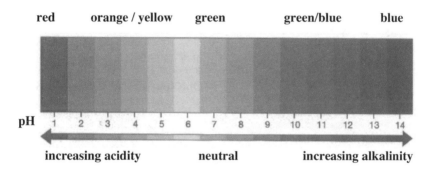

☐ Universal indicator can only measure the pH to the nearest whole number; a pH meter can be used to give a more accurate measurement of acidity and alkalinity.

☐ Some compounds called 'acids' or 'alkalis' do **not** behave as acids and alkalis unless water is present ... they only show on the pH scale when in aqueous solution,

    *e.g. dry citric acid and dry hydrogen chloride gas do **not** change the colour of dry pH paper but dissolve in Universal indicator to change the colour from green to yellow / orange / red.*

Dilution

□ A solution is formed when a substance dissolves in water.

□ A **concentrated** solution has a lot of the dissolved substance in a certain volume of water (think of concentrated orange juice); adding water **dilutes** the solution.

□ If the same volume of a concentrated and dilute solution are compared, the dilute solution will have less dissolved substance than the concentrated solution.

concentrated
solution

dilute
solution

□ In the same way, adding water to an acid or an alkali dilutes the solution; this affects both the acidity/alkalinity and the pH of the solutions.

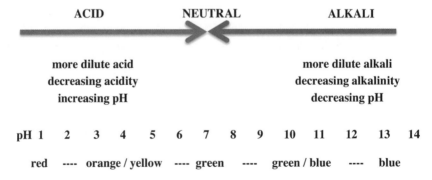

	ACID	NEUTRAL	ALKALI

more dilute acid
decreasing acidity
increasing pH

more dilute alkali
decreasing alkalinity
decreasing pH

pH 1   2   3   4   5   6   7   8   9   10   11   12   13   14

red   ----   orange / yellow   ----   green   ----   green / blue   ----   blue

Non-metal oxides

☐ An element that reacts with oxygen forms an oxide.

☐ Carbon, nitrogen and sulphur are all non-metals; carbon forms carbon dioxide (CO_2), nitrogen forms nitrogen dioxide (NO_2) and sulphur forms sulphur dioxide (SO_2).

☐ All non-metal oxides that dissolve in water form **acidic solutions**,

  e.g. the oxides of carbon, nitrogen and sulphur lower the pH of water.

☐ Sulphur dioxide is produced in the atmosphere by the burning of fossil fuels that contain sulphur, either as the element or as part of a compound; nitrogen dioxide is released into the atmosphere in car exhaust fumes; both gases dissolve in water to form an acid and when this happens in the atmosphere what is formed is known as **acid rain**, i.e. rain water (or snow, etc.) with unusually high concentrations of acid.

☐ Acid rain has a significant impact on the natural environment,

  e.g. the pH can become too low for some plants and animals in rivers and lochs to survive; forest trees can be extensively damaged; soils can become too acidic for healthy growth of plants.

☐ Acid rain also has a significant impact on structures and buildings,

  e.g. there is increased corrosion of iron (bridges, pipes, etc.) and constructions made of limestone react with acid leading to disintegration (erosion).

☐ Breathing and lung problems in children and adults who have asthma have been linked to acid rain pollution of the air.

☐ A number of steps are being taken to reduce the levels of sulphur and nitrogen oxides in the air; energy producers using fossil fuels are employing systems to trap sulphur dioxide before it is released into the atmosphere and catalytic converters in cars reduce emissions of nitrogen oxides.

☐ Since much of our energy comes from fossil fuels, reducing our use of energy can help,

  e.g. turning off lights and electrical appliances when not in use.

☐ Greater use is being made of alternative "green" energy sources,

  e.g. wind-farms.

☐ The cost of finding solutions to the acid rain problem has to be weighed against the cost of long-term damage to the world around us.

Metal oxides

☐ When a metal reacts with oxygen, the metal oxide is formed,

   e.g. sodium produces sodium oxide; calcium produces calcium oxide.

☐ All metal oxides that dissolve in water form alkaline solutions,
   i.e. increase the pH of water,

   e.g. potassium oxide and barium oxide.

☐ All metal oxides that are insoluble in water have no effect on the pH of water,

   e.g. copper(II) oxide and zinc oxide.

☐ The solubility of selected metal oxides is shown on page 5 of the Data Booklet;
   only oxides with the letter 'i' are sufficiently insoluble to have no effect on the
   pH of water ... they do **not** form an alkali (see notes on bases on page 62).

What is an acid?

☐ Hydrochloric acid, HCl (aq), nitric acid, HNO_3 (aq), and sulphuric acid,
   H_2SO_4 (aq), are common acids.

☐ The chemical formulae for each of the three acids show symbols for non-metal
   elements and this suggests that the acids are made up of molecules.

☐ However, dilute acids conduct electricity; this means that ions
   (charged particles) exist in the solutions.

☐ During electrolysis, hydrogen gas is produced at the negative electrode; this
   means that the hydrogen in an acid must exist as positive hydrogen ions,
   H^+ (aq); at the negative electrode, two hydrogen ions, $2H^+$ (aq), gain electrons
   to form uncharged hydrogen molecules.

$$2H^+ \text{(aq)} \quad + \quad 2e^- \quad \longrightarrow \quad H_2 \text{(g)}$$

☐ It is the presence of aqueous hydrogen ions, H^+ (aq), that makes a solution an
   acid.

☐ The term 'acid' is also used for compounds that do not contain H^+ (aq) ions but dissolve in water to produce H^+ (aq) ions,

e.g. hydrogen chloride gas and solid methanoic acid.

$$HCl\ (g) \quad + \quad H_2O \quad \longrightarrow \quad HCl\ (aq) \qquad [H^+\ (aq) + Cl^-\ (aq)]$$

hydrogen chloride   **hydrochloric acid**

$$HCOOH\ (s) \quad + \quad H_2O \quad \longrightarrow \quad HCOOH\ (aq) \quad [HCOO^-\ (aq) + H^+\ (aq)\ ]$$

solid   **methanoic acid**
methanoic acid

☐ The substance added is made up of molecules; when the substance dissolves in water, the covalent bonds break to form ions that become attached to water molecules, i.e. H^+ (aq) ions.

What is an alkali?

☐ Sodium hydroxide solution, NaOH (aq), potassium hydroxide solution, KOH (aq), and lithium hydroxide solution, LiOH (aq), are common alkalis.

☐ All three conduct electricity showing the presence of ions; the names and the chemical formulae indicate that the solutions contain hydroxide ions, OH^- (aq).

☐ It is the presence of aqueous hydroxide ions, OH^- (aq), that makes a solution an alkali.

☐ The term 'alkali' is also used for compounds that do not contain OH^- (aq) ions but dissolve in water to produce OH^- (aq) ions; the solid does not behave as an alkali unless water is present,

e.g. sodium hydroxide solid.

Bases

☐ Acids have a pH less than 7; alkalis have a pH greater than 7; water and neutral solutions have a pH equal to 7.

☐ Alkalis can be thought of as 'opposites' to acids because they react with acids, moving the pH towards 7 and forming water; any substance that reacts with acids in this way is called a **base**; as well as alkalis, insoluble metal hydroxides, metal oxides and metal carbonates are examples of bases.

☐ Alkalis are a subset of the set of bases; alkalis are the solutions formed when bases dissolve in water; alkalis have a pH greater than 7 due to the concentration of OH⁻ (aq).

BASES (react with acids forming water)

ALKALIS
(a solution of a base)

☐ The solubilities of metal hydroxides, metal oxides and metal carbonates are shown on page 5 of the Data Booklet; all bases, except those with an 'i', are sufficiently soluble to form an alkaline solution when added to water.

Water

☐ The chemical name for water is hydrogen oxide, H_2O; with two non-metal elements, water can be expected to be made up of molecules with the atoms joined together by covalent bonds; covalent compounds are non-conductors of electricity.

☐ A sensitive meter can be used to show that pure water does conduct electricity although very poorly; this indicates that water does not just consist of molecules ... a small number of ions must also be present in water.

☐ This is because a small number of molecules split up as follows:

$$H_2O \ (l) \longrightarrow H^+ (aq) \ + \ OH^- (aq)$$

many water
molecules   **very few ions**

☐ Since each water molecule can form one hydrogen ion, H^+ (aq), and one hydroxide ion, OH^- (aq), the concentration of H^+ (aq) in pure water is equal to the concentration of OH^- (aq); also, in a neutral solution, the concentration of H^+ (aq) is equal to the concentration of OH^- (aq).

☐ In acids, the concentration of hydrogen ions, H^+ (aq), is greater than the concentration of hydroxide ions, OH^- (aq); when an acid solution is diluted, the concentration of H^+ (aq) decreases and the concentration of OH^- (aq) increases.

☐ In alkalis, the concentration of hydroxide ions, OH^- (aq), is greater than the concentration of hydrogen ions, H^+ (aq); when an alkaline solution is diluted, the concentration of OH^- (aq) decreases and the concentration of H^+ (aq) increases.

☐ It is important to remember that all solutions in water contain both hydrogen and hydroxide ions; **it is the relative concentrations of these ions that decide whether or not a solution is acid, alkaline or neutral.**

ACID

concentration of H^+ (aq) greater than the concentration of OH^- (aq)

ALKALI

concentration of OH^- (aq) greater than the concentration of H^+ (aq)

---

10 Making salts

Neutralisation

☐ A base is a substance that reacts with an acid, decreasing the acidity; this kind of reaction is known as **neutralisation** (since the pH of the acid moves towards 7, the pH of a neutral solution).

☐ Water is one of the products of a neutralisation reaction; the other is a **salt**.

$$\text{ACID} \quad + \quad \text{BASE} \longrightarrow \text{SALT} \quad + \quad \text{WATER}$$

☐ Neutralisation of an acid involves the reaction of H^+ (aq) ions with the base.

$$H^+ \text{ (aq)} \quad + \quad \textbf{base} \longrightarrow \textbf{salt} \quad + \quad H_2O$$

☐ An alkali can also be neutralised by an acid.

$$OH^- \text{ (aq)} \quad + \quad \textbf{acid} \longrightarrow \textbf{salt} \quad + \quad H_2O$$

☐ Many neutralisation reactions occur in everyday life,

> *e.g. vinegar (acid) can be used to treat a wasp sting (alkali); indigestion tablets (alkali) are used to treat acid indigestion; lime (alkali) is used to treat acid soil.*

Naming salts

☐ In the formation of a salt by a neutralisation reaction, the aqueous hydrogen ions in the acid, H^+ (aq), are replaced by the positive metal ions (or ammonium ions) from the base; this gives the first part of the name of the salt.

☐ The second part of the name of the salt comes from the name of the negative ion in the acid.

Acid	Negative ion
hydrochloric	chloride
sulphuric	sulphate
nitric	nitrate
carbonic	carbonate
phosphoric	phosphate

> *e.g. potassium hydroxide and hydrochloric acid form potassium chloride; sodium carbonate and sulphuric acid form sodium sulphate.*

Reactions of acids

☐ Metal hydroxide solutions (alkalis), metal oxides and metal carbonates are all bases ... they react with dilute acids to form salts in a neutralisation reaction.

$$\text{ACID} \quad + \quad \text{BASE} \quad \longrightarrow \quad \text{SALT} \quad + \quad \text{WATER}$$

☐ If the base is a metal carbonate then **carbon dioxide** is also produced.

☐ The method used to make the salt depends on whether the base is soluble or insoluble in water.

(a) The reaction of acid with alkali

$$\text{ACID} \quad + \quad \text{ALKALI} \quad \longrightarrow \quad \text{SALT} \quad + \quad \text{WATER}$$

☐ This method is used when the base is **soluble** in water,

e.g. sodium chloride is prepared by the reaction of sodium hydroxide solution with dilute hydrochloric acid.

☐ An indicator has to be used to find the volume of alkali required to neutralise a known volume of acid; the experiment is repeated using the same volume of alkali without the indicator; to obtain a solid sample of the salt, the salt solution is evaporated to dryness.

(b) The reaction of an acid with a metal oxide

$$\text{ACID} \quad + \quad \text{METAL OXIDE} \quad \longrightarrow \quad \text{SALT} \quad + \quad \text{WATER}$$

☐ This method can be used when the metal oxide is **insoluble** in water,

e.g. copper(II) sulphate can be prepared by the reaction of copper(II) oxide with dilute sulphuric acid.

☐ The metal oxide will react with the acid but will not dissolve in the neutral solution; if excess metal oxide is added (more than is needed to react with all the acid), then the unreacted metal oxide can be removed from the neutral solution by filtering; the solution (the filtrate) is evaporated to dryness to obtain a solid sample of the salt.

(c) The reaction of an acid with a metal carbonate

$$\text{ACID} \quad + \quad \text{METAL CARBONATE}$$
$$\downarrow$$
$$\text{SALT} \quad + \quad \text{WATER} \quad + \quad \text{CARBON DIOXIDE}$$

☐ When the metal carbonate is **insoluble** in water, the method that can be used is the same as that for an insoluble metal oxide,

e.g. magnesium sulphate can be prepared by the reaction of magnesium carbonate with sulphuric acid.

Insoluble products

☐ Some ionic solids are soluble in water; the combination of positive and negative ions separate as the solid dissolves,

e.g. sodium chloride, Na^+Cl^- (s) and silver nitrate, $Ag^+NO_3^-$ (s).

☐ When solutions of two ionic compounds are mixed, one of the combinations of ions may be insoluble in water,

e.g. the combination of Ag^+ (aq) and Cl^- (aq) forms a solid, $Ag^+ Cl^-$ (s), whereas the combination of Na^+ (aq) and NO_3^- (aq) is soluble in water and the ions remain in solution.

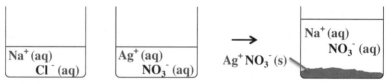

☐ The insoluble solid that settles out of the solution is called a **precipitate**; the kind of reaction that takes place is known as **precipitation**.

☐ The precipitate can be separated from the solution by filtration.

☐ The precipitate takes its name from the metal ion in one solution and the negative ion in the other.

e.g.   **silver** nitrate solution   +   sodium **chloride** solution
$$\downarrow$$
silver chloride solid   +   sodium nitrate solution

☐ The Data Booklet, page 5, can be used to find out which product, if any, will occur as a precipitate; take 'i' to be insoluble, i.e. the solid will form as a precipitate.

☐ Insoluble salts can be prepared by precipitation.

Spectator ions

☐ **Spectator ions** are ions that do not take part in a chemical reaction.

Example 1: Reaction of a dilute acid with an alkali
e.g. the reaction of sodium hydroxide solution with dilute hydrochloric acid

$$HCl\,(aq) \quad + \quad NaOH\,(aq) \quad \longrightarrow \quad NaCl\,(aq) \quad + \quad H_2O\,(l)$$

This equation can be rewritten to show the ions present.

Since water is made up almost entirely of molecules (covalent bonding) it is left unchanged.

$$H^+\,(aq) \ \text{ and } Cl^-\,(aq) \quad + \quad Na^+\,(aq) \ \text{ and } OH^-\,(aq)$$

$$\downarrow$$

$$Na^+\,(aq) \quad \text{and} \quad Cl^-\,(aq) \quad + \quad H_2O\,(l)$$

Both the Na^+ (aq) and Cl^- (aq) have not changed during the reaction. These ions are both spectator ions and can be cancelled out to show the actual reaction taking place.

$$H^+\,(aq) \ \text{ and } \cancel{Cl^-}\,(aq) \quad + \quad \cancel{Na^+}\,(aq) \ \text{ and } OH^-\,(aq)$$

$$\downarrow$$

$$\cancel{Na^+}\,(aq) \quad + \quad \cancel{Cl^-}\,(aq) \quad + \quad H_2O\,(l)$$

hence $\quad H^+\,(aq) \ + \ OH^-\,(aq) \quad \longrightarrow \quad H_2O\,(l)$

☐ The equation that shows the OH^- (aq) of the alkali reacting with the H^+ (aq) of the acid is called an **ion equation**; the ion equation shows the ions that actually take part in the reaction.

☐ The ion equation is the same for the neutralisation of any dilute acid with any alkali.

Example 2:   Reaction of a dilute acid with a metal carbonate

e.g. the reaction of dilute sulphuric acid with sodium carbonate solution

$$H_2SO_4 \,(aq) \quad + \quad Na_2CO_3 \,(aq) \longrightarrow Na_2SO_4 \,(aq) \quad + \quad H_2O \,(l) \quad + \quad CO_2 \,(g)$$

Both water and carbon dioxide are made up of molecules (covalent bonding).

Rewriting to show the ions present gives:

$2H^+$ (aq) and SO_4^{2-} (aq)   + $2Na^+$ (aq) and CO_3^{2-} (aq)

$\downarrow$

$2Na^+$ (aq) and SO_4^{2-} (aq)   + H_2O (l)   + CO_2 (g)

Both the Na^+ (aq)   and the SO_4^{2-} (aq) are spectator ions and can be cancelled out.

$2H^+$ (aq) and $\cancel{SO_4^{2-}}$ (aq)   + $2\cancel{Na^+}$ (aq) and CO_3^{2-} (aq)

$\downarrow$

$2\cancel{Na^+}$ (aq) and $\cancel{SO_4^{2-}}$ (aq)   + H_2O (l)   + CO_2 (g)

The ion equation shows what actually happens in the reaction of a dilute acid with a solution of a metal carbonate.

$$2H^+ \,(aq) \quad + \quad CO_3^{2-} \,(aq) \quad \longrightarrow \quad H_2O \,(l) \quad + \quad CO_2 \,(g)$$

Example 3: A precipitation reaction

e.g. the reaction of sodium chloride solution with silver nitrate solution

The balanced equation with state symbols is:

$$NaCl \, (aq) \quad + \quad AgNO_3 \, (aq) \quad \longrightarrow \quad NaNO_3 \, (aq) \quad + \quad AgCl \, (s)$$

In solution, the ions in an ionic compound are free to move whereas the ions in a solid are tightly packed together.

$$Na^+ \, (aq) \; \text{and} \; Cl^- \, (aq) \quad + \quad Ag^+ \, (aq) \; \text{and} \; NO_3^- \, (aq)$$

$$\downarrow$$

$$Na^+ \, (aq) \; \text{and} \; NO_3^- \, (aq) \quad + \quad Ag^+ Cl^- \, (s)$$

The spectator ions are the Na^+ (aq) and NO_3^- (aq) and these ions can be cancelled out.

$$\cancel{Na^+} \, (aq) \; \text{and} \; Cl^- \, (aq) \quad + \quad Ag^+ \, (aq) \; \text{and} \; \cancel{NO_3^-} \, (aq)$$

$$\downarrow$$

$$\cancel{Na^+} \, (aq) \; \text{and} \; \cancel{NO_3^-} \, (aq) \quad + \quad Ag^+ Cl^- \, (s)$$

hence $\qquad Cl^- \, (aq) \quad + \quad Ag^+ \, (aq) \quad \longrightarrow \quad Ag^+ Cl^- \, (s)$

This equation shows the ions that actually react.

☐ In any precipitation reaction,

$$A^+ X^- \, (aq) \quad + \quad B^+ Y^- \, (aq) \quad \longrightarrow \quad A^+ Y^- \, (s) \quad + \quad B^+ X^- \, (aq)$$

the spectator ions can be cancelled out to leave:

$$A^+ \, (aq) \quad + \quad Y^- \, (aq) \quad \longrightarrow \quad AY \, (s)$$

Volumetric titrations

☐ Acids and alkalis react to form a salt plus water in a neutralisation reaction; the concentration of acids and alkalis can be found by **volumetric titrations**.

☐ Neutralisation is complete when all of the H⁺ (aq) ions from the acid have been "cancelled out" with exactly the same number of OH⁻ (aq) ions from the alkali.

$$H^+ \text{(aq)} \quad + \quad OH^- \text{(aq)} \quad \longrightarrow \quad H_2O \text{(l)}$$

☐ The number of moles of H⁺ (aq) that react will equal the number of moles of OH⁻ (aq) that react.

☐ An indicator can be used to detect the end-point of the reaction.

☐ The actual titration is repeated a number of times to give an accurate value for the volume to be used in the calculation.

☐ The first titration is used to find the **rough** volume; with this volume known, a second and third titration can be carefully carried out, adding acid very slowly near the end-point.

☐ The actual volume used in the calculation is (usually) the average of the second and third titrations … the rough volume is ignored.

e.g.

Rough titration /cm³	Second titration /cm³	Third titration /cm³
25.6	24.5	24.3

The volume used in the calculation is **24.4 cm³**.

Example 1: Calculate the concentration of hydrochloric acid, if 20 cm³ is required to neutralise 50 cm³ of potassium hydroxide (concentration 0.1 mol l⁻¹).

$$HCl \text{(aq)} \quad + \quad KOH \text{(aq)} \quad \longrightarrow \quad KCl \text{(aq)} \quad + \quad H_2O \text{(l)}$$

Step 1   Number of moles   no. of moles   =   conc x litres
of KOH (aq)

                                                =   0.1 x 0.05

$$\boxed{n = CV}$$

                                                =   0.005 mol

| Step 2 | Use the balanced equation to find the number of moles of HCl (aq) | | 1 mol NaOH (aq) ↔ 1 mol HCl (aq) |
| | | | 0.005 mol NaOH (aq) ↔ 0.005 mol HCl (aq) |

Step 3   Calculate the concentration of HCl (aq)

$$conc = \frac{\text{no. of moles}}{\text{litres}}$$

$$\boxed{C = \frac{n}{V}}$$

$$= \frac{0.5}{2}$$

$$= \textbf{0.25 mol l}^{-1}$$

> ***Step 2 of the calculation involves simple proportion and hence the use of the ↔ symbol.***

Example 2:   **Calculate the volume of sulphuric acid (concentration 0.05 mol l⁻¹) that will neutralise 25 cm³ of sodium hydroxide solution (concentration 0.2 mol l⁻¹).**

$$H_2SO_4 \text{(aq)} + 2NaOH \text{(aq)} \longrightarrow Na_2SO_4 \text{(aq)} + 2H_2O \text{(l)}$$

Step 1   Number of moles of NaOH (aq)

$$\text{no. of moles} = conc \times litres$$

$$= 0.2 \times 0.025$$

$$\boxed{n = CV}$$

$$= 0.005 \text{ mol}$$

Step 2   Use the balanced equation to find the number of moles of H_2SO_4 (aq)

2 mol NaOH (aq) ↔ 1 mol H_2SO_4 (aq)

0.005 mol NaOH (aq) ↔ 0.0025 mol H_2SO_4 (aq)

Step 3   Calculate the volume of H_2SO_4 (aq)

$$litres = \frac{\text{no. of moles}}{conc}$$

$$\boxed{V = \frac{n}{C}}$$

$$= \frac{0.025}{0.005}$$

$$= \textbf{0.5 l } (\textbf{50 cm}^3)$$

□   The following relationship can be used to simplify calculations:

> vol x conc (mol l^{-1}) x no. of H^+ (aq) in the formula   **ACID**
> = vol x conc (mol l^{-1}) x no. of OH^- (aq) in the formula   **ALKALI**

Example 1:   Calculate the concentration of sodium hydroxide solution, if 25 cm^3 is neutralised by 50 cm^3 of hydrochloric acid (concentration 1 mol l^{-1}).

Step 1   Write relationship   vol x conc x   no. of H^+ (aq)
                                        = vol x conc x   no. of OH^- (aq)

Step 2a   Number of H^+ (aq) in   HCl (aq) = 1
             formula of acid

Step 2b   Number of OH^- (aq) in   NaOH (aq) = 1
             formula of alkali

Step 3   Put in variables   50 x 1 x 1 = 25 x c x 1

Step 4   Complete calculation   concentration = **2 mol l^{-1}**

Example 2:   Calculate the volume of sulphuric acid (concentration 0.05 mol l^{-1}) that will neutralise 25 cm^3 of potassium hydroxide solution (concentration 0.1 mol l^{-1}).

Step 1   Write relationship   vol x conc x   no. of H^+ (aq)
                                        = vol x conc x   no. of OH^- (aq)

Step 2a   Number of H^+ (aq) in H_2SO_4 (aq) = 2
             formula of acid

Step 2b   Number of OH^- (aq) in   KOH (aq) = 1
             formula of alkali

Step 3   Put in variables   vol x 0.05 x 2 = 25 x 0.1 x 1

Step 4   Complete calculation   volume = **25 cm^3**

1 Fuels

Sources of energy ***

☐ A **fuel** is any material that has stored energy that can be used for a particular purpose; much of our energy comes from burning fuels to produce heat,

   e.g. wood was one of the first fuels used by humans.

☐ The **burning** of a fuel is a chemical reaction in which energy (mainly heat) is released.

☐ The oxygen of the air is required for a fuel to burn ... the fuel is used up as it reacts with the oxygen of the air to make new substances (the products of the reaction).

☐ **Combustion** is another word for burning.

☐ **Fossil fuels** are formed from the remains of ancient plants and animals; over many millions of years these remains are covered by layers of rock and the exposure to high heat and pressure in the Earth's crust results in the formation of the fuels,

   e.g. coal, oil and natural gas are fossil fuels.

☐ The energy in fossil fuels can be traced back to the Sun; it is stored in plants during **photosynthesis**, a biological process; by eating food of plant-origin, the energy is transferred to animals.

☐ The burning of fossil fuels releases the Sun's energy from plants and animals that were living many millions of years ago.

Fire triangle ***

☐ The fire triangle indicates that there are three 'requirements' for most fires; these are **heat**, **fuel** and **oxygen**; a fire naturally occurs when heat, fuel and oxygen are combined in the right way; the fire goes out by removing any one of them.

HEAT · FUEL · OXYGEN

- [ ] Without sufficient heat, a fire cannot begin, and it cannot continue; a fire can be put out by the application of a substance that takes heat from the fire,

  e.g. adding water removes heat as water is changed to steam; scraping away red-hot ash from a burning fire removes the heat source.

- [ ] Without fuel, a fire will stop.

  e.g. fuel is removed naturally when the fire is burning; controlled burning of trees to remove fuel is an essential part of forest management where forest fires are likely.

- [ ] Without sufficient oxygen, a fire cannot begin, and it cannot continue; with a decreased oxygen concentration, the combustion process slows; in most cases, there is plenty of air left when the fire goes out so this is commonly not a major factor.

Burning fossil fuels ***

- [ ] A **hydrocarbon** is a compound containing carbon and hydrogen **only**; fossil fuels are mainly hydrocarbons with minor impurities,

  e.g. natural gas is mainly methane, a hydrocarbon with the chemical formula CH_4.

- [ ] 'Burning fossil fuels' means that hydrocarbon molecules are reacting with the oxygen molecules of the air; the products of the reaction are carbon dioxide and water ... the oxides of the elements that make up the hydrocarbon; energy, mainly heat, is also given out.

- [ ] The apparatus shown can be used to collect the products from the burning of hydrocarbons for identification.

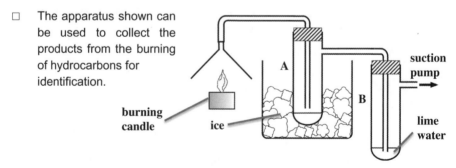

- [ ] A colourless liquid condenses in test-tube **A**; the liquid has a melting point of 0 °C and a boiling point of 100 °C; this is water.

- [ ] The lime water in test-tube **B** turns milky due to carbon dioxide being produced.

Complete and incomplete combustion ***

☐ Fossil fuels (hydrocarbons) burn to produce carbon dioxide and water; for these products to form, a good air supply is needed; this is **complete combustion**.

　e.g. **lighter fuel　　+　　oxygen　　⟶　　carbon dioxide　+　　water**

☐ Carbon monoxide and carbon can be produced where the supply of oxygen (from the air) is limited; this is **incomplete combustion**; with incomplete combustion, the hydrogen from the hydrocarbon still forms water.

　e.g. there is incomplete combustion of petrol and diesel in car engines.

　　petrol　+　　oxygen　　⟶　　carbon monoxide (or **carbon**)　+　　**water**

☐ When a beaker of water is heated by burning Bunsen gas with the air-hole closed, a black solid is observed on the underside of the beaker; this is carbon, formed because the hydrocarbons in the gas are burning in a limited supply of oxygen.

Air pollution ***

☐ Air pollution is a result of impurities in the air; most of the pollutants come from burning hydrocarbon fuels,

　e.g. gas, oil, petrol and diesel from crude oil (see notes on fractional distillation on page 79).

☐ Air pollution is therefore more of a problem in industrial areas; as well as damaging the environment, pollution is a health hazard,

　e.g. pollutant gases can contribute to lung disease and bronchitis.

☐ When a hydrocarbon fuel burns completely, the carbon atoms in the hydrocarbon molecules react with the air to form carbon dioxide; however, incomplete combustion produces **carbon monoxide**, a poisonous gas; carbon monoxide reacts with haemoglobin in blood, stopping it carrying oxygen to the brain and other parts of the body.

☐ Crude oil contains small amounts of sulphur; the burning of fuels from crude oil produces **sulphur dioxide**; this gas dissolves in rain to form acid rain.

☐ **Nitrogen dioxide** is also found in car exhaust fumes; nitrogen and oxygen of the air do not normally react but the spark that ignites the petrol can provide the energy to produce a reaction; nitrogen dioxide also dissolves in rain water to form acid rain.

Reducing air pollution ***

☐ Car exhaust systems can be fitted with a catalytic converter; these systems contain transition metals that act as a catalyst for the reaction of harmful carbon monoxide and nitrogen dioxide to harmless carbon dioxide and nitrogen.

☐ Another way of decreasing air pollution due to carbon monoxide is to improve the efficiency of combustion; this can be done by increasing the air to fuel ratio; the higher concentration of oxygen is more likely to lead to complete combustion and a consequent decrease in the formation of carbon and carbon monoxide.

☐ Sulphur compounds can be removed from petrol; these can be used to manufacture sulphuric acid, a very important chemical.

Finite energy sources ***

☐ **Finite sources of energy** are sources of energy that, having been used up, cannot be replaced; all fossil fuels are finite sources of energy,

e.g. coal, oil and natural gas.

☐ Over-use of fossil fuels in order to satisfy the energy demands of the industrial world may lead to a fuel crisis.

☐ **Renewable sources of energy** can constantly be replaced,

e.g. wind, tidal and solar energy.

☐ **Biomass** is the term given to plant- or animal-based material, i.e. material from living or recently living organisms (from 'bio' meaning living).

☐ Since biomass is produced from a carbon source that can be replaced, biomass is a renewable source of energy.

☐ In the first instance, biomass can be used as a fuel,

e.g. burning logs from dead trees.

☐ Biomass can also be used produce **biofuels**,

e.g. crops such as sugar-cane can be grown to produce ethanol, a fuel that can be used in place of petrol; biodiesel, another useful fuel, can be produced from waste vegetable oils and animal fats.

The carbon cycle ***

☐ There are millions and millions of carbon atoms in all living things; carbon atoms, joined to atoms of other elements as part of compounds, are also found in the ground, in the sea and also in the air (as carbon dioxide).

☐ The carbon atoms do not stay in the same place ... they constantly move round as a result of various processes,

e.g. *we put carbon from glucose molecules in our bodies into the atmosphere as carbon dioxide when we breathe out.*

☐ The movement of carbon from one place to another is referred to as the **carbon cycle**.

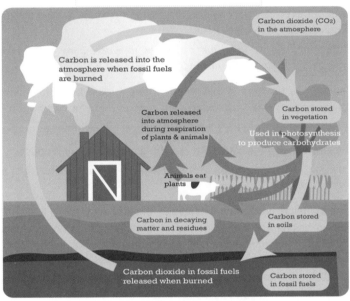

from Earth Science in Maine

The greenhouse effect ***

☐ Some gases in the atmosphere act like the glass in a greenhouse; they trap heat, keeping the Earth warm enough for plants and animals to survive; these gases are called **greenhouse gases**,

e.g. carbon dioxide is one of the important greenhouse gases.

☐ In many industrial areas of the world, there is significantly more carbon dioxide being released into the atmosphere through the burning of fossil fuels; some scientists believe that greatly increased levels of carbon dioxide may be causing the Earth to heat up, an effect called **global warming**.

☐ Changes to climate may be a result of global warming.

☐ Many of our everyday actions will (directly or indirectly) involve the production of carbon dioxide from fossil fuels,

e.g. cars and buses, used for travelling to work, burn fossil fuels; using electricity produced by burning fossil fuels.

☐ The carbon we produce in this way (as carbon dioxide) is sometimes called our **carbon footprint**; calculating our carbon footprint can help us to think about our contribution to global warming and climate change.

☐ Businesses can also calculate the carbon footprint for their products,

e.g. the carbon produced (as carbon dioxide) in the manufacture of a television or a computer.

☐ In some industrial processes that involve the burning of fossil fuels, the carbon dioxide emissions are separated from the other gases; once separated, the carbon dioxide is compressed and transported to a suitable site for geological storage; there it is injected into deep underground rock formations, often at depths of more than one kilometre; the whole process, known as **carbon capture and storage** (**CCS**), may be important in reducing levels of carbon dioxide and hence responding to the challenges presented by global warming.

Distillation ***

☐ **Distillation** is a way of separating a mixture of liquids by using the difference in boiling points.

☐ The process of distillation involves:
   * heating a liquid until it boils to form a gas;
   * cooling the gas somewhere else to allow it to condense back into the liquid.

☐ The piece of apparatus used to condense the gas back into the liquid is called a **condenser**.

☐ A mixture of alcohol and water is separated by distillation in the manufacture of whisky; the alcohol (boiling point 78 °C) boils off first.

☐ The salt and water in a salt solution can also be separated by distillation; this happens in desalination plants that are used to produce drinking water from sea water.

Fractional distillation of crude oil ***

☐ Crude oil is found under the ground or the sea-bed; it is a mixture of many different liquids and dissolved solids and gases.

☐ Although this mixture of compounds is not of immediate use, crude oil is a source of many useful fuels.

☐ The fuels that are obtained from crude oil are all fossil fuels and so they are all mixtures of hydrocarbons.

☐ To be of use, the oil has to be separated into **fractions** that contain compounds of roughly the same boiling point; this process is called **fractional distillation**.

☐ Although each one is still a mixture of compounds, a fraction can be used directly as a fuel.

☐ Much of the crude oil that is used in the UK comes from the North Sea; however, crude oil also comes from other countries,
   e.g. in the Gulf area in the Middle East, Russia, Alaska, Nigeria, etc.

☐ The percentage of the different fractions depends on the source of the crude oil.

☐ The table below shows a use for the different fractions obtained from crude oil.

	Gas	Petrol (naphtha)	Kerosene (paraffin)	Diesel	Residue
Use	fuel	fuel for cars	heating fuel, aviation fuel	fuel for cars and lorries	road tar
Number of carbon atoms	1-4	4-10	9-16	15-25	25+
Boiling point range/ °C	-160 to 20	20 to 120	120 to 240	240 to 350	over 350

☐ There are observable differences across the fractions.

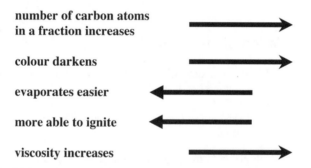

number of carbon atoms in a fraction increases

colour darkens

evaporates easier

more able to ignite

viscosity increases

The viscosity of a liquid is its ease of flow, i.e. more viscous liquids flow like treacle rather than like water.

2 Structure of hydrocarbons

Hydrocarbons

☐ A **hydrocarbon** is a compound made up of **only** hydrogen and carbon atoms, *e.g. hexane, C_6H_{14}, is a hydrocarbon but acetone, C_3H_6O, is **not** a hydrocarbon because acetone contains atoms of oxygen as well.*

☐ Since both carbon and hydrogen are non-metal atoms, hydrocarbons are made up of molecules with the atoms joined by covalent bonds, i.e. by the sharing of electron pairs.

☐ Carbon is in Group 4 of the Periodic Table and so atoms of carbon have four electrons in the outer shell (energy level).

☐ With four 'extra' electrons in the outer shell, carbon atoms have the stable electron arrangement of the nearest noble gas (neon) and so, in hydrocarbons, carbon atoms form four covalent bonds with either other carbon atoms or hydrogen atoms.

☐ Hydrogen atoms have one electron in the first shell.

☐ With one 'extra' electron in the outer shell, hydrogen atoms have the stable electron arrangement of the nearest noble gas (helium) and so, in hydrocarbons, hydrogen atoms form one covalent bond with carbon atoms.

Methane, ethane and propane

☐ The hydrocarbon with just one carbon atom is called **methane**.

☐ In a molecule of methane, one carbon atom is joined to four hydrogen atoms to give a stable electron arrangement for all the atoms in the molecule.

☐ The formula for methane is CH_4; this gives the number of atoms of each element in the molecule but CH_4 does not give any information about the arrangement of atoms in the molecule; information about the arrangement of atoms is given by the **full structural formula**.

$$H-\overset{\overset{\displaystyle H}{|}}{\underset{\underset{\displaystyle H}{|}}{C}}-H$$

☐ The full structural formula is 'flat'; the actual structure of methane is based on the three-dimensional tetrahedral arrangement of electrons in a carbon atom:

☐ Molecules of **ethane** have two carbon atoms joined by a single covalent bond.

$$C-C$$

☐ Each carbon atom can form three bonds with hydrogen atoms.

$$H-\overset{\overset{\displaystyle H}{|}}{\underset{\underset{\displaystyle H}{|}}{C}}-\overset{\overset{\displaystyle H}{|}}{\underset{\underset{\displaystyle H}{|}}{C}}-H$$

☐ Molecules of **propane** have three carbon atoms joined by single covalent bonds.

$$C-C-C$$

☐ Three hydrogen atoms are attached to the end carbon atoms; two hydrogen atoms are attached to the middle carbon atom.

$$H-\overset{\overset{\displaystyle H}{|}}{\underset{\underset{\displaystyle H}{|}}{C}}-\overset{\overset{\displaystyle H}{|}}{\underset{\underset{\displaystyle H}{|}}{C}}-\overset{\overset{\displaystyle H}{|}}{\underset{\underset{\displaystyle H}{|}}{C}}-H$$

☐ Like methane, ethane and propane molecules are three-dimensional; the bonds around each carbon atom point towards the corners of a tetrahedron.

The alkanes

☐ Methane, ethane and propane are the first three members of a series of hydrocarbons called the **alkanes**; the alkanes are a subset of the set of hydrocarbons.

☐ Each member of the alkane series has a name that ends in –**ane** and a prefix that indicates the number of carbon atoms in the molecule,

Prefix	Number of carbon atoms in the molecule
meth -	1
eth -	2
prop -	3
but -	4
pent -	5
hex -	6
hept -	7
oct -	8

e.g. methane is the alkane with one carbon atom per molecule.

☐ All the hydrocarbons in the alkane series are known as **saturated** hydrocarbons; a saturated hydrocarbon is one in which all the carbon to carbon bonds are single covalent bonds.

☐ A shortened structural formula can be used to show the grouping of hydrogen atoms round each carbon atom; the different ways of representing the alkanes with one to six carbon atoms are shown below.

Name	Full structural formula	Shortened structural formula	Formula
methane	$H-\overset{\displaystyle H}{\underset{\displaystyle H}{C}}-H$	CH_4	CH_4
ethane	$H-\overset{\displaystyle H}{\underset{\displaystyle H}{C}}-\overset{\displaystyle H}{\underset{\displaystyle H}{C}}-H$	CH_3-CH_3	C_2H_6
propane	$H-\overset{\displaystyle H}{\underset{\displaystyle H}{C}}-\overset{\displaystyle H}{\underset{\displaystyle H}{C}}-\overset{\displaystyle H}{\underset{\displaystyle H}{C}}-H$	$CH_3-CH_2-CH_3$	C_3H_8
butane	$H-\overset{\displaystyle H}{\underset{\displaystyle H}{C}}-\overset{\displaystyle H}{\underset{\displaystyle H}{C}}-\overset{\displaystyle H}{\underset{\displaystyle H}{C}}-\overset{\displaystyle H}{\underset{\displaystyle H}{C}}-H$	$CH_3-CH_2-CH_2-CH_3$	C_4H_{10}
pentane	$H-\overset{\displaystyle H}{\underset{\displaystyle H}{C}}-\overset{\displaystyle H}{\underset{\displaystyle H}{C}}-\overset{\displaystyle H}{\underset{\displaystyle H}{C}}-\overset{\displaystyle H}{\underset{\displaystyle H}{C}}-\overset{\displaystyle H}{\underset{\displaystyle H}{C}}-H$	$CH_3-CH_2-CH_2-CH_2-CH_3$	C_5H_{12}
hexane	$H-\overset{\displaystyle H}{\underset{\displaystyle H}{C}}-\overset{\displaystyle H}{\underset{\displaystyle H}{C}}-\overset{\displaystyle H}{\underset{\displaystyle H}{C}}-\overset{\displaystyle H}{\underset{\displaystyle H}{C}}-\overset{\displaystyle H}{\underset{\displaystyle H}{C}}-\overset{\displaystyle H}{\underset{\displaystyle H}{C}}-H$	$CH_3-CH_2-CH_2-CH_2-CH_2-CH_3$	C_6H_{14}

,

Ethene and propene

☐ Carbon atoms can also join up by the sharing of two electron pairs, i.e. by forming two covalent bonds.

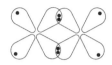

☐ The two covalent bonds between two carbon atoms is called a **double covalent bond**.

$$C=C$$

☐ Each carbon atom can only form two bonds with other atoms

$$\diagdown C = C \diagup$$

☐ The hydrocarbon with two carbon atoms joined by a double covalent bond is called **ethene**.

$$\begin{array}{c} H \diagdown \quad \diagup H \\ C=C \\ H \diagup \quad \diagdown H \end{array}$$

☐ Molecules of **propene** have three carbon atoms joined by covalent bonds; one is a double covalent bond.

$$\underset{1 \quad 2 \quad 3}{C=C-C}$$

☐ Two hydrogen atoms are attached to carbon atom 1; one hydrogen atom is attached to carbon atom 2; three carbon atoms are attached to carbon atom 3.

$$\begin{array}{c} \qquad H \quad H \\ H \diagdown \quad | \quad | \\ C=C-C-H \\ H \diagup \, 1 \quad 2 \quad |3 \\ \qquad \qquad H \end{array}$$

The alkenes

☐ Ethene and propene are the first two members of a series of hydrocarbons called the **alkenes**; the alkenes are another subset of the set of hydrocarbons.

☐ Each member of the alkene series has one carbon to carbon double bond.

☐ The name ends in **–ene** and a prefix (same as for alkanes) indicates the number of carbon atoms in the molecule,

e.g. ethene is the alkene with two carbon atoms per molecule.

☐ All the hydrocarbons in the alkene series are known as **unsaturated** hydrocarbons; an unsaturated hydrocarbon has (at least) one carbon to carbon double bond in each molecule.

☐ The different ways of representing the alkenes with two to six carbons are shown below.

Name	Full structural formula	Shortened structural formula	Formula
ethene	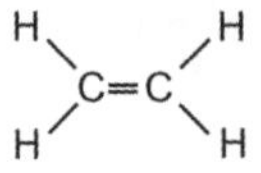 H, H $C=C$ H, H	$CH_2{=}CH_2$	C_2H_4
propene	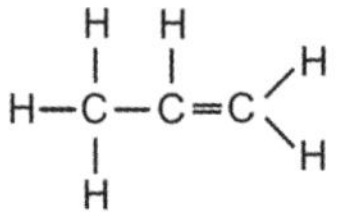 H H $H{-}C{-}C{=}C$ H, H	$CH_3{-}CH{=}CH_2$	C_3H_6
butene	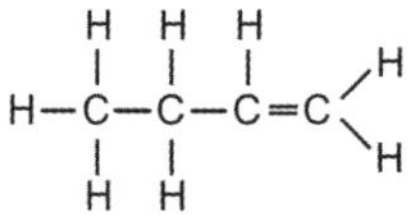 H H H $H{-}C{-}C{-}C{=}C$ H, H	$CH_3{-}CH_2{-}CH{=}CH_2$	C_4H_8
pentene	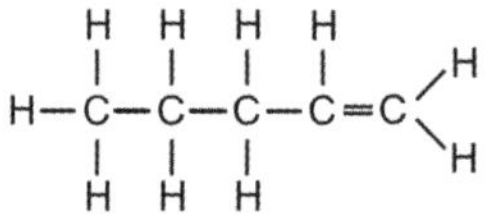 H H H H $H{-}C{-}C{-}C{-}C{=}C$ H, H	$CH_3{-}CH_2{-}CH_2{-}CH{=}CH_2$	C_5H_{10}
hexene	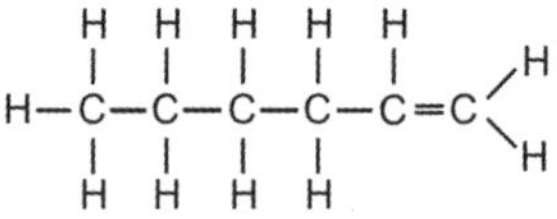 H H H H H $H{-}C{-}C{-}C{-}C{-}C{=}C$ H, H	$CH_3{-}CH_2{-}CH_2{-}CH_2{-}CH{=}CH_2$	C_6H_{12}

The cycloalkanes

☐ Carbon atoms can join together with covalent bonds to form closed chains or 'rings'; alkanes with a ring of carbon atoms are called **cycloalkanes**.

☐ Cycloalkanes are another subset of the set of hydrocarbons; each member of the cycloalkane series has a name beginning with '**cyclo**' to indicate that there is a ring of carbon atoms.

☐ The name ends in –**ane** to indicate that all the carbon to carbon bonds are single covalent bonds and a prefix (same as for alkanes) indicates the number of carbon atoms in the molecule.

☐ The first member of the series is **cyclopropane** with three carbon atoms joined in a ring by single covalent bonds.

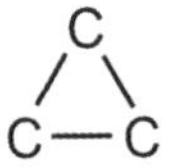

☐ Each carbon atom is able to form two covalent bonds with hydrogen atoms.

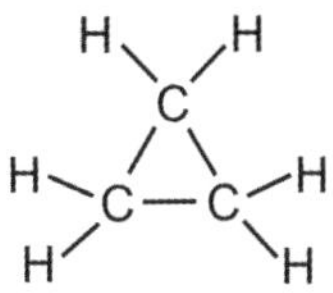

☐ The different ways of representing the cycloalkanes with three to six carbon atoms are shown below.

Name	Full structural formula	Shortened structural formula	Formula
cyclopropane	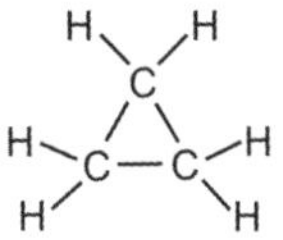	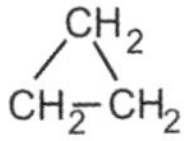	C_3H_6
cyclobutane	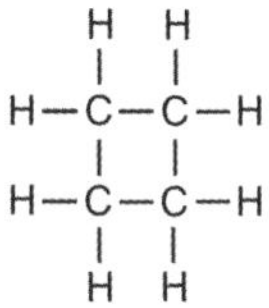	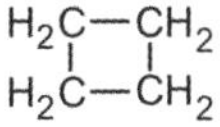	C_4H_8
cyclopentane	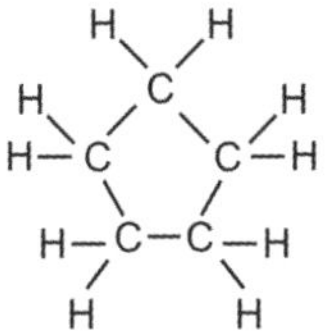	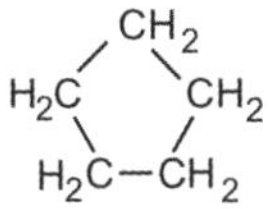	C_5H_{10}
cyclohexane	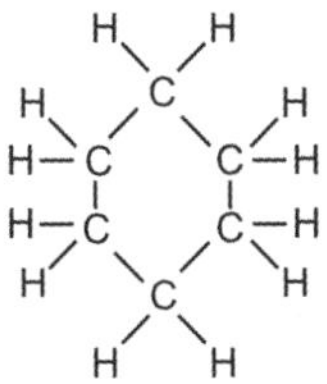	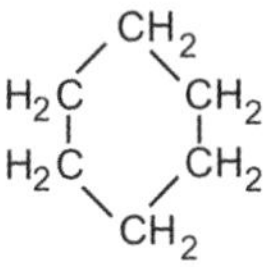	C_6H_{12}

Homologous series

☐ A homologous series is a family of compounds that can be represented by a general formula.

☐ The general formula for the **alkanes** is C_nH_{2n+2}; each of the alkanes has two hydrogen atoms for every carbon atom plus one additional hydrogen at each end.

☐ The general formula for the **alkenes** is C_nH_{2n}; each of the alkenes has two hydrogen atoms less than the alkanes due to the double (rather than the single) covalent bond.

☐ The general formula for the **cycloalkanes** is also C_nH_{2n}; each of the cycloalkanes has two hydrogen atoms less than the corresponding alkane due to the bond that closes the ring.

☐ Successive members in a series differ in formula by a $-CH_2$ group and as a result the relative formula masses differ by 14.

☐ Physical properties show a gradual change from one member to the next,

   e.g. boiling point.

☐ Chemical properties of compounds in the one homologous series are very similar,

   e.g. all alkenes react with bromine.

☐ However, chemical properties can be used to distinguish between hydrocarbons in different series,

   e.g. although alkenes and cycloalkanes have the same general formula, alkenes react with bromine but cycloalkanes do not (see notes on reactions of alkenes on page 94).

Naming alkanes

☐ Carbon compounds are given a systematic name according to an internationally accepted convention.

☐ There are three different structures for the compound with molecular formula C_5H_{12}; their shortened structural formulae are shown below.

A $\quad CH_3-CH_2-CH_2-CH_2-CH_3$

B $\quad CH_3-CH-CH_2-CH_3$
$\qquad\qquad |$
$\qquad\quad\; CH_3$

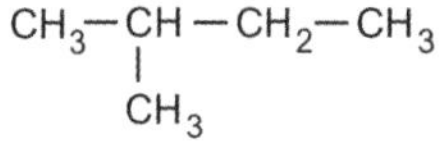

C $\quad \begin{array}{c} CH_3 \\ | \\ CH_3-C-CH_3 \\ | \\ CH_3 \end{array}$

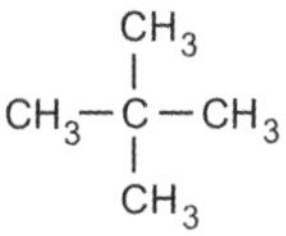

Structure **A** is called a **straight chain** hydrocarbon; structures **B** and **C** are called **branched chain** hydrocarbons.

☐ Branches are named after the corresponding alkanes with the –ane ending changed to -yl.

e.g.

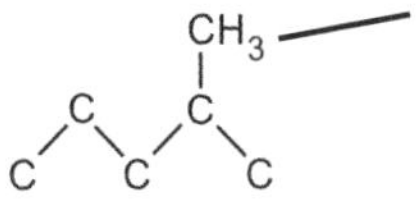

methyl group

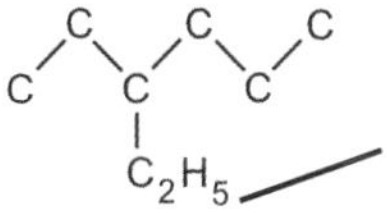

ethyl group

☐ To name an alkane:

1. Select the longest continuous chain of carbon atoms and name it after the appropriate alkane.
2. Number the carbon atoms from the end of the chain nearer the branch.
3. Name the branch(es) and indicate the position(s) of the branch(es) on the chain with the number(s) of the carbon atoms(s).
4. Use 'di' and 'tri', etc. when the same branch is present more than once.

e.g.

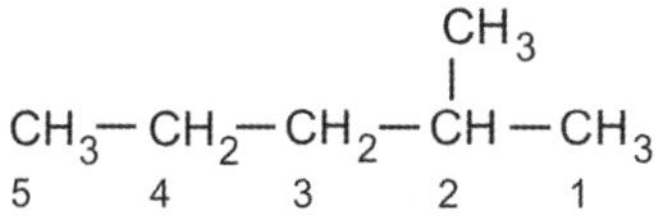

$\qquad\qquad\qquad\qquad CH_3$
$\qquad\qquad\qquad\qquad\;\; |$
$CH_3-CH_2-CH_2-CH-CH_3$
$\;\, 5 \quad\;\; 4 \quad\;\; 3 \quad\;\; 2 \quad\;\; 1$

2-methylpentane

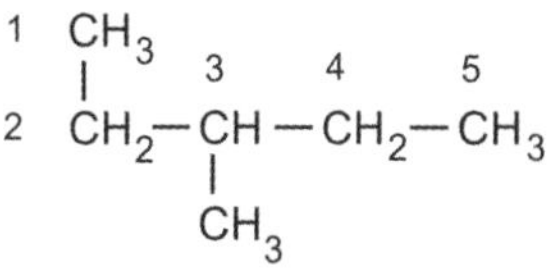

$\;\; 1\;\; CH_3$
$\qquad\;\; | \qquad 3 \qquad 4 \qquad 5$
$\;\; 2\;\; CH_2-CH-CH_2-CH_3$
$\qquad\qquad\quad |$
$\qquad\qquad\;\; CH_3$

3-methylpentane

$\qquad\;\; CH_3 \quad CH_3$
$\qquad\;\; | \qquad\;\; |$
$CH_3-CH-CH-CH_3$
$\; 4 \quad\;\; 3 \quad\;\; 2 \quad\;\; 1$

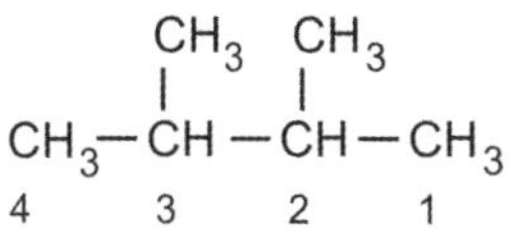

2,3-dimethylbutane

Naming alkenes

☐ Alkenes are named in a similar way to alkanes.

1 Select the longest continous chain of carbon atoms containing the double bond and name it after the appropriate alkene.

2. Number the carbon atoms from the end of the chain nearer the double bond and indicate the position of the double bond with the lowest number of carbon atom at the double bond.

3. Name any branch(es) and indicate the position(s) of the branch(es) on the chain with the number(s) of the carbon atom(s).

e.g. $CH_3-CH_2-CH=CH_2$ $CH_3-CH=CH-CH_3$
        4   3   2   1   4   3   2   1

         but-1-ene   **but-2-ene**

$$CH_3$$
$$|$$
$$CH_2=CH-CH-CH_3$$
  1   2   3   4

3-methylbut-1-ene

Isomers

☐ **Isomers** are compounds with the same molecular formula but different structures.

☐ The following flow diagram can be used to decide whether or not two compounds are isomers.

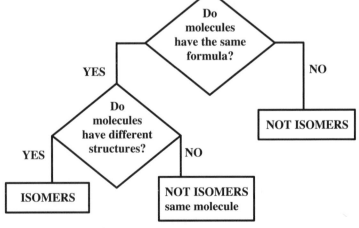

Examples:

1. $CH_3-CH_2-CH_3$ CH_3-CH_3 **different formulae**
       propane   ethane   **NOT isomers**

2. $CH_3-CH_2-CH_2-CH_3$ CH_3-CH_2 **same formula**
                                    $\quad\quad\; |$ **same structure**
                                    $\quad\quad CH_2-CH_3$ **NOT isomers**
       butane   butane

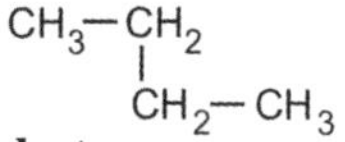

3. $\quad\; CH_3$ $CH_3-CH_2-CH-CH_3$ **same formula**
       $\quad\;\; |$ $\quad\quad\quad\quad |$ **same structure**
       $CH_3-CH-CH_2-CH_3$ $\quad\quad\quad CH_3$ **NOT isomers**

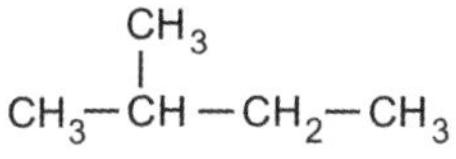

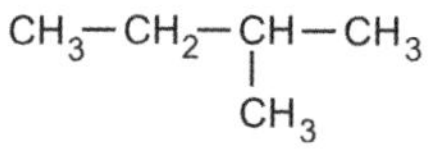

       methylbutane   methylbutane

> *Name is written as methylbutane – number not necessary.*

4. $\quad\;\; CH_3$ $CH_3-CH-CH_2-CH_3$ **same formula**
       $\quad\quad |$ $\quad\quad |$ **different structures**
       CH_3-C-CH_3 $\quad\quad CH_3$ **isomers**
       $\quad\quad |$
       $\quad\;\; CH_3$
       dimethylpropane   methylbutane

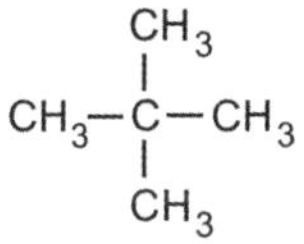

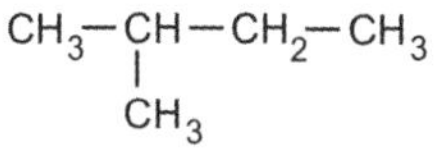

> *Names are written as dimethylpropane and methylbutane*
> *- number(s) not necessary.*

5. $CH_2{=}CH-CH_2-CH_3$ $CH_3-CH{=}CH-CH_3$ **same formula**
                                                            different structures
       but-1-ene   but-2-ene   **isomers**

6. $CH_2{=}CH-CH_2-CH_3$ $CH_3-CH_2-CH{=}CH_2$ **same formula**
                                                            same structure
       but-1-ene   but-1-ene   **NOT isomers**

7. $CH_3-CH{=}CH_2$ $\quad CH_2$ **same formula**
                                    $\quad /\;\; \backslash$ **different structures**
       propene $CH_2{-}CH_2$ **isomers**

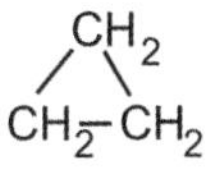

                                    cyclopropane

☐ Many carbon compounds, other than hydrocarbons, have isomers.

Examples:

1.

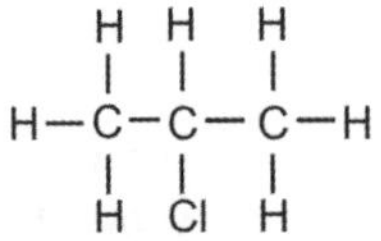

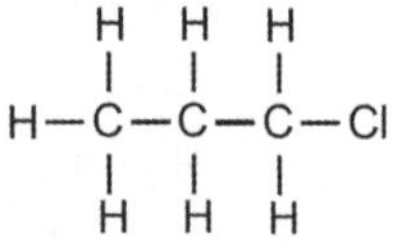

$$H-\underset{\underset{H}{|}}{\overset{\overset{H}{|}}{C}}-\underset{\underset{Cl}{|}}{\overset{\overset{H}{|}}{C}}-\underset{\underset{H}{|}}{\overset{\overset{H}{|}}{C}}-H \qquad H-\underset{\underset{H}{|}}{\overset{\overset{H}{|}}{C}}-\underset{\underset{H}{|}}{\overset{\overset{H}{|}}{C}}-\underset{\underset{H}{|}}{\overset{\overset{H}{|}}{C}}-Cl$$

**same formula
different structures
isomers**

2.

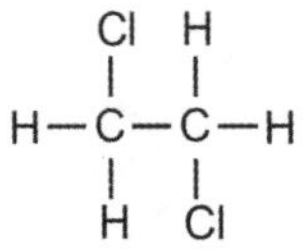

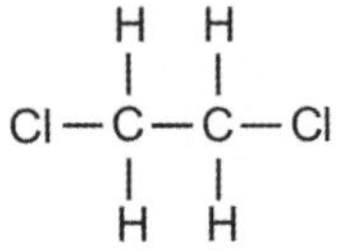

$$H-\underset{\underset{H}{|}}{\overset{\overset{Cl}{|}}{C}}-\underset{\underset{Cl}{|}}{\overset{\overset{H}{|}}{C}}-H \qquad Cl-\underset{\underset{H}{|}}{\overset{\overset{H}{|}}{C}}-\underset{\underset{H}{|}}{\overset{\overset{H}{|}}{C}}-Cl$$

**same formula
same structure
NOT isomers**

3. $CH_3-O-CH_3 \qquad CH_3-CH_2-OH$

**same formula
different structures
isomers**

3 Reactions of hydrocarbons

Cracking ***

☐ Crude oil is a source of fuels,

e.g. petrol, kerosene and diesel.

☐ However the process of fractional distillation of crude oil does not produce sufficient petrol to meet present day demands; on the other hand, there is a surplus of the 'heavier' fuels like kerosene and diesel.

☐ **Cracking** is an industrial process that breaks up (cracks) the larger molecules in the heavier fractions into petrol; when a catalyst is used to bring this about the process is called **catalytic cracking**.

☐ Decreasing the temperature of an industrial reaction is likely to reduce the cost of the process (less energy required); however, decreasing the temperature slows down the speed of a chemical reaction ... but in the presence of a catalyst the reaction can still proceed at an acceptable rate at a lower temperature.

☐ Cracking can be carried out in the lab.

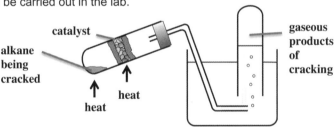

☐ When the gaseous products are tested with bromine solution, the solution is immediately decolourised showing that (at least) one of the products of cracking an alkane is unsaturated.

☐ When the cracking of an alkane molecule produces two products, one will be saturated and the other will be unsaturated; there are not enough hydrogens to give two smaller alkane molecules.

e.g. C_8H_{18} $\longrightarrow$ C_6H_{12} + C_2H_6

         octane   **hexene**   **ethane**

     large molecule   smaller molecule   smaller molecule
      (saturated)   (unsaturated)   (saturated)

☐ The total number of carbon and hydrogen atoms in the product molecules always add up to the number of carbon and hydrogen atoms in the reactant molecule.

☐ All the carbon bonds in an alkane are equally strong; any can be broken in the cracking process; as a result, cracking always produces a mixture of products.

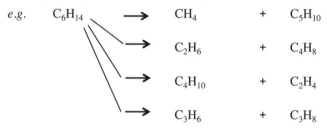

e.g. $\quad C_6H_{14} \quad \longrightarrow \quad CH_4 \quad + \quad C_5H_{10}$

$\longrightarrow \quad C_2H_6 \quad + \quad C_4H_8$

$\longrightarrow \quad C_4H_{10} \quad + \quad C_2H_4$

$\longrightarrow \quad C_3H_6 \quad + \quad C_3H_8$

☐ In some cases, cracking produces more than two products.

e.g. $\quad C_{16}H_{34} \quad \longrightarrow \quad C_6H_{14} \quad + \quad C_3H_6 \quad + \quad C_7H_{14}$

$\quad\quad\quad\quad\quad\quad\quad\quad$ **hexane** $\quad\quad\quad$ **propene** $\quad\quad$ **heptene**

Reactions of alkenes

☐ Alkanes and cycloalkanes are **saturated** hydrocarbons; all the carbon to carbon bonds are **single covalent bonds**.

☐ Alkenes are **unsaturated** hydrocarbons; the molecules contain one carbon to carbon **double covalent bond**.

☐ When bromine (in solution) is added to an unsaturated hydrocarbon, the brown colour of the bromine 'disappears', i.e. the bromine is immediately decolourised (it is incorrect to say that the bromine solution goes clear … it is clear to begin with); there is no immediate reaction when bromine is added to a saturated hydrocarbon.

☐ In the reaction of bromine with the unsaturated hydrocarbon, the carbon to carbon double bond breaks and the bromine atoms add on the carbon atoms at either side of this bond.

e.g. **ethene with bromine**

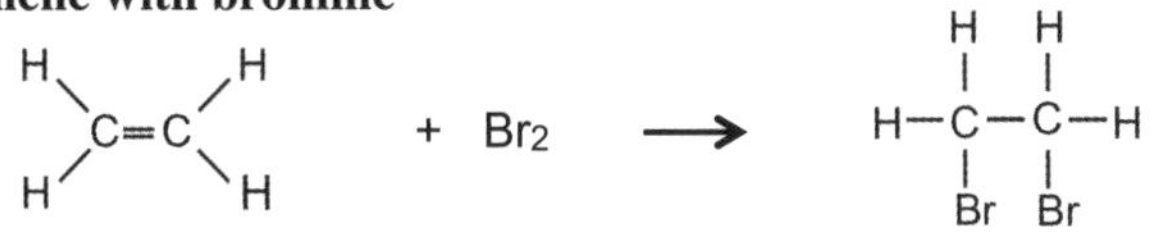

propene with bromine

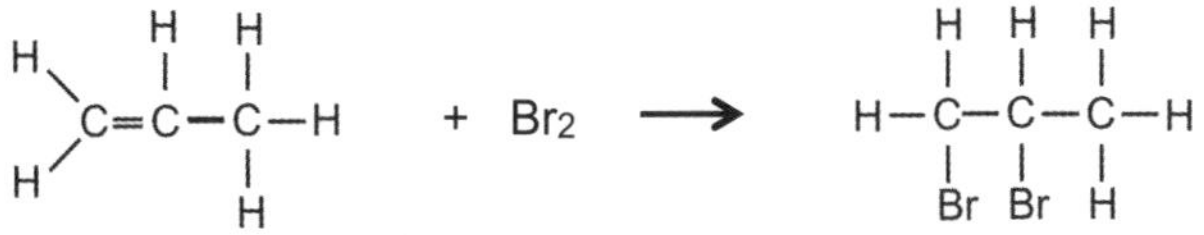

☐ This kind of reaction is called an **addition reaction** because of the way that bromine adds on to the alkene.

☐ The reaction with bromine is the way to distinguish an unsaturated hydrocarbon from a saturated hydrocarbon; the bromine is immediately decolourised by the unsaturated hydrocarbon.

☐ Alkenes can also react with hydrogen in an addition reaction; the corresponding alkane is formed,

e.g. **ethene with hydrogen**

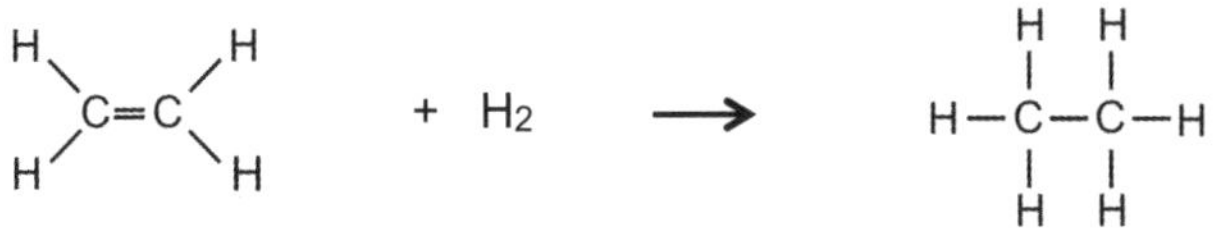

ethane

4 Carbohydrates

Carbohydrates ***

☐ Many of our foods contain a class of compound called **carbohydrates**,
e.g. 'starchy' foods like potatoes, pasta and bread; 'sugary' foods like sweets.

☐ The elements in a carbohydrate can be worked out from the name:
carbo - for carbon
hydrate – for hydrogen and oxygen (from the Greek word for water)

☐ However, the hydrogen and oxygen atoms in carbohydrates are not present as water molecules … but the two elements are present in the same ratio as in water, i.e. two hydrogen atoms for every one oxygen atom.

☐ Carbon, hydrogen and oxygen are non-metal elements and so carbohydrates are made up of molecules with atoms joined by covalent bonds.

Respiration ***

☐ When a carbohydrate burns, it reacts with the oxygen of the air to form carbon dioxide and water; a lot of energy is released in the process.

☐ In the lab, when carbohydrate powder burns in a large tin can, the energy is sufficient to 'blow' the lid of the can.

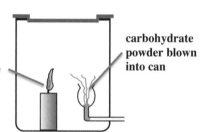

carbohydrate powder blown into can

candle

☐ Glucose is a carbohydrate that we obtain from our food.

☐ In our bodies, glucose 'burns-up' in a similar way to the burning carbohydrate in the lab but much more slowly; the energy is produced over a much longer period of time; this process is known as **respiration**.

oxygen

glucose

ENERGY

water

carbon dioxide

☐ When we blow through a straw into a test tube of lime water, the lime water turns milky showing there is carbon dioxide in the air we breathe out.

☐ When we blow onto a test tube of ice, water from the air we breathe out forms on the outside of the cold test tube; breathing onto a cold window in winter has the same effect.

☐ Respiration takes place in all our living cells and the energy coming from the process is used in a wide variety of ways,

  e.g. to keep us warm, to keep the muscles working so that we can move about.

☐ The process of respiration is common to all animals; respiration also takes place in plants but only when the plants are in the dark.

Photosynthesis ***

☐ All animals require glucose from foods to give them energy; these foods come from plants.

☐ Glucose is produced in plants by a process called photosynthesis.

☐ A clue to the meaning comes from the name:
  photo – light   **synthesis** – building up

☐ In the process of photosynthesis, water (taken in by the roots) reacts with carbon dioxide (taken in from the air through the leaves); oxygen is also produced in the process.

☐ Without photosynthesis there would be no oxygen for animals to breathe in for respiration.

chlorophyll in plant leaves

carbon dioxide

oxygen

glucose

water

☐ The energy that is stored in the carbohydrate molecules that are built up as a result of photosynthesis comes from the light of the Sun; the light is 'trapped' by **chlorophyll**, the green coloured substance in plants that is essential for the process.

Maintaining the balance ***

☐ Life as we know it would not be possible without respiration and photosynthesis; these two processes keep a balance between levels of oxygen and carbon dioxide in the atmosphere.

☐ During the hours of daylight, plants photosynthesise using the Sun's energy.

carbon dioxide + water + energy ⟶ glucose + oxygen

☐ By this process, plants provide both energy-producing foods and oxygen for animals.

☐ The reverse of photosynthesis is respiration, a reaction that provides energy for animals.

glucose + oxygen ⟶ carbon dioxide + water + energy

☐ Human activity has interfered with the balance between the levels of carbon dioxide and oxygen in the air,

e.g. the increased burning of fossil fuels, particularly in industrial areas, gives higher levels of carbon dioxide; the clearing of large forests decreases the levels of carbon dioxide that can be used in photosynthesis.

☐ As a result, the levels of carbon dioxide in the atmosphere are higher than before; this build up may be responsible for the rising temperature of the Earth, i.e. global warming, and hence climate change.

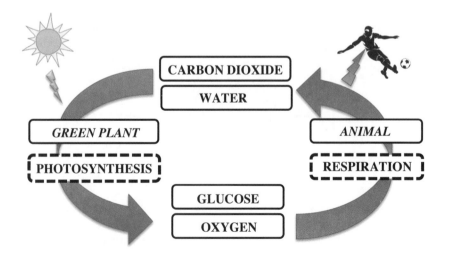

Starch and glucose ***

- [ ] Starch and glucose are both carbohydrates; they are both made up of carbon, hydrogen and oxygen atoms (the hydrogen and oxygen in the ratio of two to one) but they have quite different structures.

- [ ] Unlike starch, glucose has a sweet taste just like ordinary sugar; however, in the interest of safety, we cannot use taste to distinguish between starch and glucose in the lab!

- [ ] Glucose dissolves in water to form a colourless solution; starch does **not** dissolve in water to form a solution … the solid particles are 'suspended' in the water; the suspension of a solid in a liquid is known as a **colloid**.

- [ ] There is a clear difference when test tubes of glucose solution and starch in water are held in a beam of light.

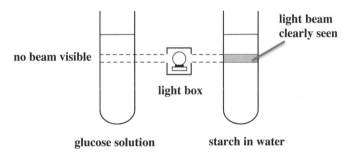

no beam visible

light beam clearly seen

light box

glucose solution   starch in water

- [ ] Starch particles are too small to be seen by the naked eye but large enough to reflect a beam of light.

- [ ] Many substances form a colloid in water; although this can be used to distinguish starch from glucose, this cannot be used as a test for starch.

Testing for starch and glucose ***

- [ ] Chemical tests are needed to distinguish starch from glucose and to identify each from other white powders.

- [ ] **Iodine solution** is used to test for starch; the iodine solution changes from a brown colour to blue / black in the presence of starch.

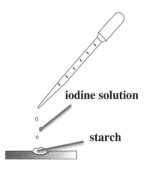

iodine solution

starch

- **Benedict's solution** is used to test for glucose; when heated, the Benedict's solution changes from a blue colour to orange/red in the presence of glucose; a water bath is used to give an even and gentle heat.

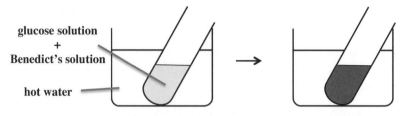

- Foods that contain starch include bread, potatoes and pasta; foods with high levels of glucose include citrus fruits, tomatoes, honey and sweets.

Making starch ***

- All plants take in carbon dioxide from the air and water molecules through the roots from the soil and use them to make glucose molecules; they do this by the process of photosynthesis.

- The energy that is stored in the glucose molecules comes from the light of the Sun; the light is 'trapped' by chlorophyll, the green coloured substance in plants that is essential for photosynthesis.

- Plants do not store energy in the form of glucose ... they do this in the form of starch; carbohydrate foods that are 'rich' in starch can supply us with glucose for the process of respiration.

- Glucose molecules are (relatively) small; starch molecules are very large ... many thousands of glucose molecules are needed to make one starch molecule.

- Starch is formed from glucose by a type of reaction known as **polymerisation**; in this type of reaction, huge numbers of small molecules join together to form very large molecules; the small molecule (glucose) is known as a **monomer** and the large molecule formed (starch) is known as a **polymer**.

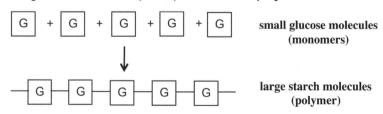

Breaking down of starch ***

☐   Animals require glucose for respiration.

      glucose   +   oxygen   ⟶   carbon dioxide   +   water

☐   Glucose can be obtained from foods containing starch; starch is a polymer
made from glucose and during digestion the starch is broken down in our
bodies to the smaller glucose molecules.

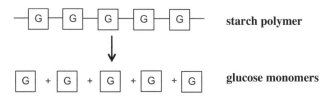

    starch polymer

    glucose monomers

☐   The glucose molecules are sufficiently small to be able to pass through the gut
wall to be used in cells throughout the body in respiration.

☐   Starch can be broken down to make glucose in the lab by amylase, an enzyme
found in saliva; visking tubing can be used to model what happens at the gut
wall; the glucose molecules can be detected in the 'outside' solution using
Benedict's solution.

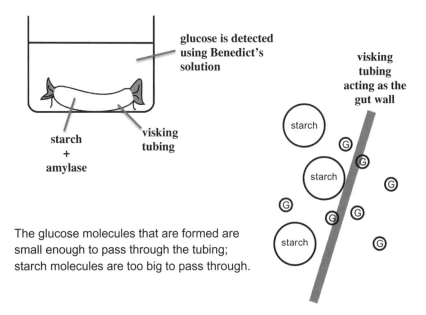

**glucose is detected
using Benedict's
solution**

**visking
tubing
acting as the
gut wall**

**starch
+
amylase**

**visking
tubing**

☐   The glucose molecules that are formed are
small enough to pass through the tubing;
starch molecules are too big to pass through.

Alcoholic drinks ***

☐ Alcohol, for alcoholic drinks, can be made by the **fermentation** of glucose; an enzyme in yeast acts as a catalyst for the reaction. Carbon dioxide gas is also produced in the process.

glucose ⟶ alcohol + carbon dioxide

☐ The glucose can come from any fruit or vegetable that is a source of carbohydrate; the type of alcoholic drink varies with the plant source of the carbohydrate.

Source	Drink
grape	wine
barley	beer, whisky
apples	cider
potatoes	vodka

☐ The alcohol content of drinks is measured in units of alcohol.

Drink	Alcohol content in units
pint of beer/lager	approx. 2.5
small glass of wine	approx. 2
large glass of wine	approx. 3
single measure of spirit	approx. 1
bottle of alcopop	approx. 1.5

☐ Alcohol is a sedative and slows down the nervous system; this can lead to loss of control and can affect balance; a high intake of alcohol can result in unconsciousness and even death; long term abuse of alcohol can cause cirrhosis of the liver.

☐ For health reasons, it is advised that we should not regularly drink more than the daily unit guidelines; for men, this is 3 to 4 units of alcohol and for women this is 2 to 3 units of alcohol.

☐ At concentrations above about 15%, the alcohol poisons the living organisms in the yeast, the catalyst in the fermentation process; there is therefore a limit to the alcohol concentration of fermentation products.

☐ **Distillation** is a method of separating liquids because of the difference in boiling points.

☐ Water and alcohol can be separated in this way ... alcohol (b.p. 78 °C) boils off first.

☐ Distillation is the process used to increase the alcohol concentration of fermentation products in the manufacture of 'spirit' drinks, *e.g. gin, vodka, whisky.*

Enzyme efficiency ***

☐ An enzyme is a biological catalyst.

☐ The rate of the catalysed reaction is related to the efficiency of an enzyme.

☐ The efficiency of enzymes are affected by changes in pH and temperature.

☐ The enzyme is most efficient, i.e. rate is fastest, under **optimum** conditions; optimum pH values and optimum temperatures vary from one enzyme to another.
e.g.

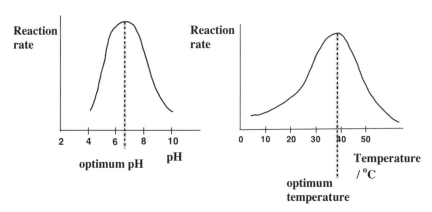

☐ Enzymes that work in the body have an optimum temperature of around 37 °C (body temperature).

5 Alcohols, carboxylic acids and esters

The alcohols

☐ Alcohol is found in alcoholic drinks; however, more than one carbon compound can be classified as an alcohol; like the alkanes, alkenes and cycloalkanes, the **alcohols** make up a homologous series.

☐ Ethanol ('eth-' meaning two carbon atoms) is the alcohol found in alcoholic drinks.

☐ The **hydroxyl group** (-OH) is the group that gives the characteristic properties to the alcohols; the atoms in a hydroxyl group are joined by a covalent bond and the group is part of a covalent molecule (compare with the hydroxide ion OH^- (aq) found in alkalis; see notes on page 61).

☐ Each member of the alcohol series has a name that ends in -**anol** and a prefix that indicates the number of carbon atoms in the molecule,

   e.g. ethanol has the hydroxyl group attached to two carbon   C—C—OH
   atoms as shown.

☐ The different ways of representing ethanol are shown below.

Full structural formula	Shortened structural formula	Formula

H H
  | |
H—C—C—OH
  | |
H H
	$CH_3\text{-}CH_2\text{-}OH$	C_2H_5OH

☐ Ethanol can be prepared in industry by the reaction of ethene with water; since the double bond breaks as the atoms in water are added on to the carbon atom at either side, this is another example of an **addition** reaction.

$$ \text{ethene} \qquad + \qquad \text{water} \qquad \longrightarrow \qquad \text{ethanol} $$

☐ This kind of reaction is also known as **hydration**.

☐ It is different from hydrolysis since the atoms of water are added to the one molecule without the molecule splitting into two parts (see notes on esters on page 109).

Naming alcohols

☐ From propanol onwards, isomerism can occur due to different positions of the hydroxyl group.

e.g.

$$\overset{3}{C}H_3-\overset{2}{C}H_2-\overset{1}{C}H_2-OH \qquad \overset{1}{C}H_3-\overset{2}{\underset{\underset{OH}{|}}{C}H}-\overset{3}{C}H_3$$

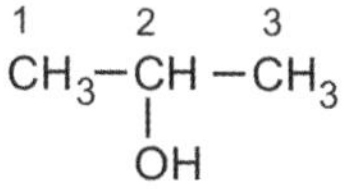

☐ To name an isomeric alcohol:

1 Select the longest continuous chain of carbon atoms containing the hydroxyl group and name it after the appropriate alcohol.

2 Number the carbon atoms from the end of the chain nearer the hydroxyl group and indicate the position of the group.

3 Name any branch(es) and indicate the position(s) of the branch(es) on the chain.

e.g.

$$CH_3-CH_2-CH_2-OH \qquad CH_3-\underset{\underset{OH}{|}}{CH}-CH_3$$

propan-1-ol   **propan-2-ol**

$$CH_3-\underset{\underset{CH_3}{|}}{CH}-CH_2-CH_2-OH$$

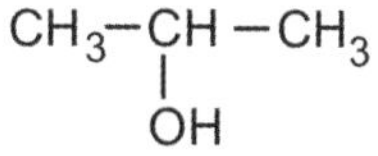

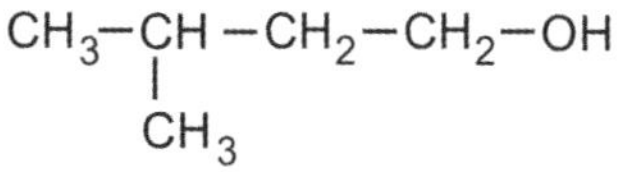

3-methylbutan-1-ol

☐ Some alcohols have more than one hydroxyl group.

e.g.

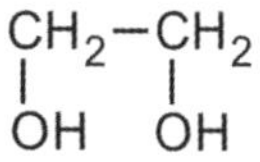

$$\underset{\underset{OH}{|}}{CH_2}-\underset{\underset{OH}{|}}{CH_2} \qquad \underset{\underset{OH}{|}}{CH_2}-\underset{\underset{OH}{|}}{CH}-\underset{\underset{OH}{|}}{CH_2}$$

ethane-1,2-diol   **propane-1,2,3-triol**

(ethylene glycol,   **(glycerol)**

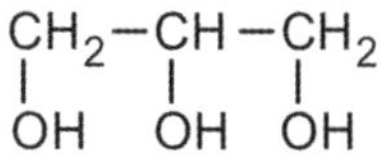

found in antifreeze)

Carboxylic acids

☐ Vinegar is an acidic solution; ethanoic acid is the name of the solution that gives vinegar the sour taste.

☐ Ethanoic acid ('eth' meaning two carbon atoms) is the second member of another homologous series called the **carboxylic acids.**

☐ The group that gives the characteristic properties to the carboxylic acids is the **carboxyl** group:

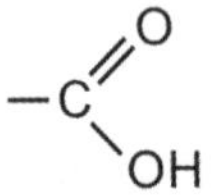

$$-C \overset{\displaystyle O}{\underset{\displaystyle OH}{\Big\backslash}}$$

☐ Each member of the carboxylic acid homologous series has a name that ends in -**anoic acid** and a prefix that indicates the number of carbon atoms in the molecule,

e.g. ethanoic acid has two carbon atoms including the carbon in the carboxylic acid group.

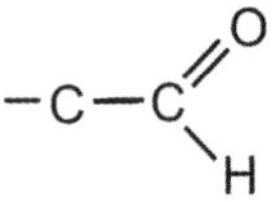

$$-C-C \overset{\displaystyle O}{\underset{\displaystyle H}{\Big\backslash}}$$

☐ The characteristic acid group must always be at the end of a carbon chain.

☐ The different ways of representing ethanoic acid are shown below.

Full structural formula	Shortened structural formula	Formula
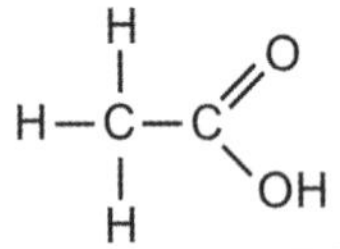 $H-\overset{\displaystyle H}{\underset{\displaystyle H}{C}}-C\overset{O}{\underset{OH}{}}$	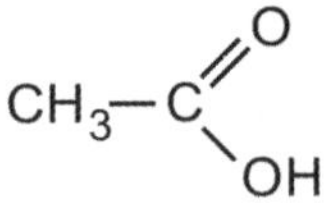 $CH_3-C\overset{O}{\underset{OH}{}}$	CH_3COOH

☐ With branched chain carboxylic acids, any branch(es) and the position(s) of the branch(es) on the chain are named in the same way as with alcohols.

e.g.

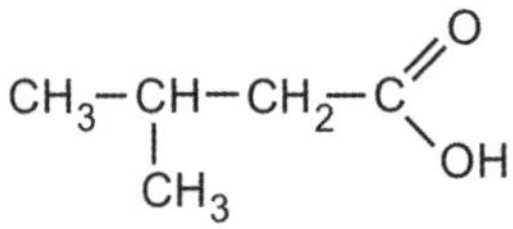

$$CH_3-\underset{\underset{\displaystyle CH_3}{|}}{CH}-CH_2-C\overset{O}{\underset{OH}{}}$$

3-methylbutanoic acid

$$CH_3-CH_2-\underset{\underset{\displaystyle CH_3}{|}}{CH}-C\overset{O}{\underset{OH}{}}$$

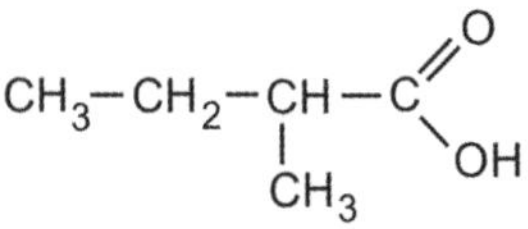

2-methylbutanoic acid

Esters

☐ **Esters** are covalent compounds with the molecules containing carbon, hydrogen and oxygen atoms.

☐ Esters have characteristic smells and are insoluble in water.

☐ Esters are the products of reactions between alcohols and carboxylic acids.

☐ An ester takes its name from the alcohol and carboxylic acid from which it can be made; the name contains the ending **-yl** (from the alcohol) and **-oate** (from the carboxylic acid); the alcohol part of the name always comes first.

> *e.g.*   alcohol: methanol   acid: ethanoic
>
>   ester: **methyl**   ester: **ethanoate**
>
>   name: **methyl ethanoate**

☐ Since esters are prepared from alcohols and carboxylic acids, all esters contain the characteristic group:

from acid 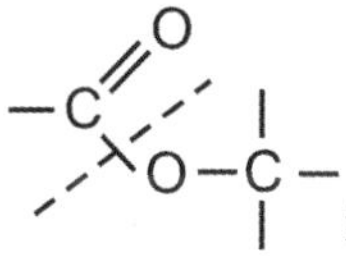
from alcohol

> *Note that the alcohol part of the structure has been turned round.*

☐ When written the other way round, the group looks like:

from alcohol 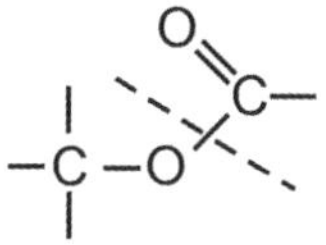
from acid

> *Note that the acid part of the structure has been turned round.*

☐ Esters can be named from their structure; the side of the structure with the $\diagdown$C=O must come from the acid.

e.g.

from alcohol   **from acid**

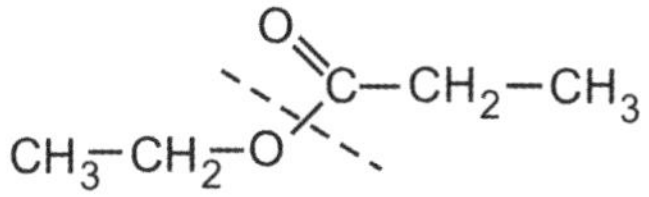

> alcohol: ethanol   acid: propanoic
>
> ester: **ethyl**   ester: **propanoate**
>
> name: **ethyl propanoate**

from acid

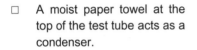

from alcohol

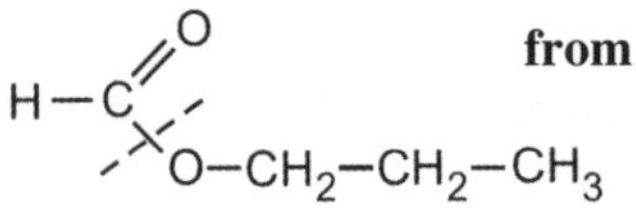

alcohol: propanol   acid: methanoic

ester: **propyl**   ester: **methanoate**

name: **propyl methanoate**

☐ Esters can be prepared in the lab by heating the alcohol and the acid with concentrated sulphuric acid; the concentrated sulphuric acid acts as a catalyst for the reaction.

☐ A moist paper towel at the top of the test tube acts as a condenser.

☐ A hot water bath is used rather than a Bunsen burner since the alcohol is flammable.

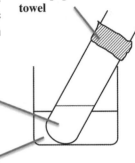

moist paper towel

alcohol
+
carboxylic acid
+
concentrated sulphuric acid

hot water

Making and breaking esters

☐ Esters are the products of reactions between alcohols and carboxylic acids,

e.g. the reaction between ethanoic acid and methanol can be represented:

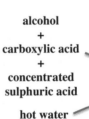

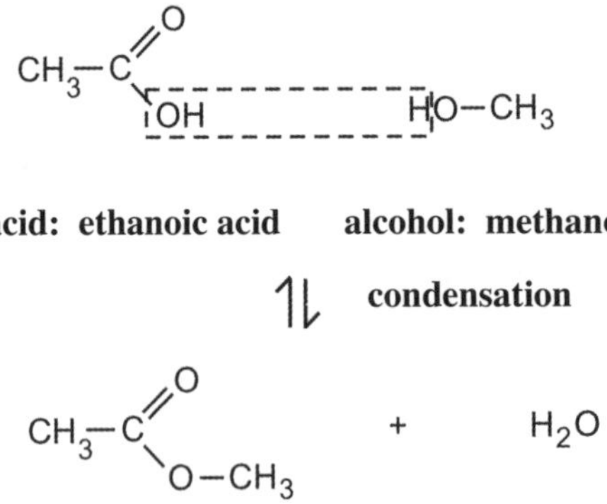

acid: ethanoic acid   **alcohol: methanol**

⇅ **condensation**

CH_3-C 〈$^O_{O-CH_3}$〉   + H_2O

ester: methyl ethanoate

☐ This kind of reaction is called a **condensation** reaction, since two reactants join up with the elimination of the atoms to make water; the reaction is also referred to as **esterification.**

☐ The ' ⇌ ' sign shows that the making of an ester is a **reversible** reaction; in a reversible reaction, the products formed in the forward reaction can react to return to the starting substances in a reverse reaction.

☐ In the reverse of a condensation reaction, esters can be broken down to the alcohol and carboxylic acid by heating with an acid or an alkali.

☐ The ester always breaks in the middle of the molecule.
  e.g.

$$CH_3-CH_2-C\overset{\displaystyle O}{\underset{\displaystyle O-CH_3}{}} \qquad + \qquad H_2O$$

ester: methyl propanoate

⇟ **hydrolysis**

$$CH_3-CH_2-C\overset{\displaystyle O}{\underset{\displaystyle OH}{}} \qquad + \qquad HO-CH_3$$

acid: propanoic acid   **alcohol: methanol**

☐ This kind of reaction is called a **hydrolysis** reaction (the breakdown of the ester to give smaller molecules occurs due to the addition of the atoms present in water).

☐ It is different from hydration since there is a splitting of the molecules as a result of the addition (see notes on page 108).

☐ The breakdown of an ester is also a reversible reaction.

Uses of carbon compounds

☐ Alcohols are often effective solvents for substances that are insoluble in water.

☐ Alcohols with smaller molecules evaporate easily, making then ideal for cleaning solvents; methylated spirits (or meths) is ethanol mixed with other chemicals; in some cases it is also dyed.

☐ The high flammability and the very clean flame with which they burn has resulted in alcohols being used as fuels; ethanol is mixed with petrol for use as an engine fuel in countries where the alcohol can be economically produced in sufficient quantities,

  e.g. in Brazil.

☐ Ethanol can be obtained by the fermentation of sugar cane which can be considered as a renewable source of energy.

☐ Methanol is also used as a fuel; it is a safer fuel in motor car racing where crashes and fires are more likely.

☐ Vinegar is a solution of ethanoic acid.

☐ Vinegar is used as a preservative in the food industry; foods in vinegar can be stored for a long time because the low pH prevents the growth of harmful bacteria and fungi.

☐ Vinegar is also used in household cleaning products designed to remove the build-up of insoluble carbonates found on plumbing fixtures,

  e.g. taps.

☐ The ethanoic acid reacts with the carbonates in a neutralisation reaction (see notes on page 66).

☐ Esters are made up of molecules that evaporate relatively easily; as a result, some uses of esters are based on their characteristic smells,

  e.g. in fragrances.

☐ Like alcohols, esters are good solvents for many substances that are insoluble in water,

  e.g. nail varnish remover, model glues and paints.

6 Energy from fuels

Energy changes

☐ An **exothermic reaction** is one in which energy is released,

e.g. when a fuel burns (combustion), heat is given out and so the surroundings become warmer; when an acid is added to an alkali, the temperature of the solution rises.

☐ The flame in a Bunsen burner is a result of burning methane, i.e. methane and oxygen reacting to form carbon dioxide and water.

$$CH_4 \quad + \quad 2O_2 \quad \longrightarrow \quad CO_2 \quad + \quad 2H_2O$$

☐ In the chemical reaction, energy is required to break the covalent bonds in the reactant molecules ... to overcome the forces of attraction holding the atoms in the molecules together.

☐ New covalent bonds can then be formed in the product molecules; when these are formed, energy is released.

☐ In a reaction in which energy is released, i.e. an exothermic reaction, more energy is given out in the bond making than is required for bond breaking.

☐ The opposite of an exothermic reaction is an **endothermic reaction** ... one in which energy is taken in during the reaction and the surroundings cool down,

e.g. when solid ammonium nitrate and hydrated barium hydroxide are mixed in a flask the temperature falls; if the flask is placed on a block of wood on which a few drops of water have been placed, the decrease in temperature is sufficient to freeze the water and the flask 'sticks' to the block.

☐ In a reaction in which energy is taken in, i.e. an endothermic reaction, more energy is taken in when bonds break than is given out in bond making.

Energy from fuels

☐ Alkanes and alcohols can be used as fuels,

e.g. natural gas is mainly methane; ethanol is mixed with petrol for use in cars.

☐ The energy released in the burning of a fuel can be calculated by using the heat energy to raise the temperature of a known mass of water.

The heat released, E_h = $c \, m \, \Delta T$

Where c = specific heat capacity of water

= $4.18 \text{ kJ kg}^{-1}\,{}^{\circ}\text{C}^{-1}$

m = mass of water absorbing heat in kg

ΔT = temperature change

1000 cm³ of water has a mass of 1kg.

Example: **Calculate the heat released on the burning of a fuel that raises the temperature of 100 cm³ of water by 10.5 °C.**

$$E_h = c \, m \, \Delta T$$
$$= 4.18 \times 0.1 \times 10.5$$
$$= 4.39 \text{ kJ}$$

☐ In the lab, the calculated energy released is less than the actual energy released because some energy is lost to the surroundings,

e.g. the container for the water and the air.

☐ The energy released from the burning of different fuels can be compared by calculating the energy released for the burning of one mole of each.

Alcohol	Structural formula	Heat released / kJ mol^{-1}
methanol	CH_3OH	727
ethanol	$CH_3 \, CH_2OH$	1367
propan-1-ol	$CH_3 \, CH_2 \, CH_2OH$	2020

☐ There is a fairly constant difference between the heat released per mole for any two successive members of a homologous series; since each pair differ by a -CH2 group, the difference in heat released is approximately constant.

Calculations based on equations

☐   A balanced equation gives information about the relative quantities involved in the reaction; this is expressed in terms of the relative number of moles of each reactant and product.

☐   Since the mass of one mole of any substance is the formula mass in grams, the masses involved can then be calculated.

Example 1: Calculate the mass of water produced on burning 1 g of methane.

Step 1 Balanced equation CH_4 + $2O_2$ $\longrightarrow$ CO_2 + $2H_2O$

Step 2 Relative number   1 mol   2 mol
         of moles

> *It is not necessary to calculate the masses of carbon dioxide and oxygen as these substances are not included in the question.*

Step 3 Find the formula masses CH_4 H_2O

                                   $12 + (1 \times 4)$ $(1 \times 2) + 16$

                                        $= 16$ $= 18$

Step 4 Mass in grams   16 g   18 g

Step 5 Multiply by the number   16 g   2 x 18 g
         of moles   = 36g

Step 6 Complete calculation   16 g $\leftrightarrow$ 36 g

                                        1 g $\leftrightarrow$ $\dfrac{36 \times 1}{16}$

$$= \mathbf{2.25\ g}$$

> *The last part of the calculation involves simple proportion and hence the use of the $\leftrightarrow$ symbol.*

Example 2: An industrial plant produces ammonia, NH_3, from nitrogen and hydrogen. An output of 7.5×10^3 kg of ammonia is required each day.

Calculate the daily mass of nitrogen needed for this output to be achieved.

Step 1	Balanced equation	$N_2 + 3H_2 \longrightarrow 2NH_3$	
Step 2	Relative number of moles	1 mol	2 mol
Step 3	Find the formula masses	14 x 2	14 + (1 x 3)
		= 28	= 17
Step 4	Mass in grams	28 g	17 g
Step 5	Multiply by the number of moles	28 g	2 x 17 g
			= 34 g
Step 6	Complete calculation	28 g ↔	34 g

$$\frac{28 \times 7.5 \times 10^3}{34} \quad \longleftrightarrow \quad 7.5 \times 10^3$$

$$= \mathbf{6.18 \times 10^3 \, kg}$$

There is no need to change kg into g in this kind of calculation.
The unit in the answer will always be the same as the unit given in the question ... this could be g, kg or even tons.
In the example above, the question indicates an output of 7.5×10^3 kg and this is used in the calculation in step 6 - hence the answer is in kg.

---

1 Metals

Metals ***

☐ It is very hard to imagine a world without metals; they are used to make so many different things, from bridges and cars to cans and nails.

☐ Metals are elements; there are close to eighty in the Periodic Table; all but one are solid at room temperature ... the exception is mercury.

☐ The uses of a metal are related to its properties,

e.g. iron (in the form of steel) is strong and used to make bridges and buildings; aluminium is used to make saucepans because it is a good conductor of heat.

Mixtures ***

☐ Many metallic objects are not made of pure metal ... a metal is mixed with one or more other elements; such a mixture is called an **alloy**.

☐ An alloy can be a mixture of metals or metals mixed with other non-metallic elements.

☐ By changing the composition of the mixture, it is possible to control the properties of the alloy; this makes alloys more useful than pure metals.

☐ Many thousands of alloys are now made; most of these have been designed with specific properties to do a particular job,

e.g. solder, a mixture of lead and tin, has a low melting point and is used to join metal pieces together in electrical circuitry.

Reducing the waste ***

☐ The metals we use come from the Earth's crust; only a few metals are not joined up with other elements ... most metals are only found in naturally occurring metal compounds called **ores**.

☐ Before these metals can be used, they have to be taken from their ores; this process is called **extraction**.

☐ Like gas, oil and coal, metals are examples of a **finite resource**; the supply from the ground will eventually run out.

☐ Many things made of metal are thrown away after being used only once,

 e.g. food and drink containers.

☐ The waste can be reduced by **recycling** the metals; instead of throwing waste metal away, it can be collected and re-used; as well as saving valuable resources, energy is saved because it is much cheaper to produce metal from scrap than to extract it from an ore.

Metallic bonding

☐ The electrons in the outermost shells (energy levels) of metal atoms are not tightly held in position ... the metal atoms contribute these electrons to a common 'pool' of free or **delocalised electrons**.

☐ The structure of metals may therefore be regarded as a regular array of positively charged ions in a sea of delocalised electrons; each positively charged ion is attracted to the pool of negative electrons and vice versa; these electrostatic attractions, which constitute the metallic bond, hold the entire metal crystal together as a single unit.

☐ The electrons in the pool do **not** belong to particular ions; when a voltage is applied, they are free to move from one ion to another throughout the metal lattice ... this is why metals conduct electricity.

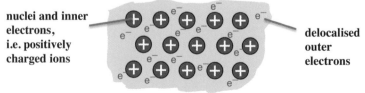

nuclei and inner electrons, i.e. positively charged ions

delocalised outer electrons

Chemistry in Society

2 Reactions of metals

Reaction with oxygen

☐ Some metals react very easily with other substances … these metals are reactive; a metal that is not very reactive (inactive) does **not** react readily with other substances.

☐ Most metals react with oxygen; the products of such reactions are compounds that are called metal oxides.

$$\textbf{metal} \quad + \quad \textbf{oxygen} \quad \longrightarrow \quad \textbf{metal oxide}$$

☐ The alkali metals are stored under oil because they are very reactive metals and react relatively fast with the oxygen of the air; these metals are not suitable as materials for everyday objects.

☐ With less reactive metals, the reaction with oxygen may not be immediately obvious because of the slowness of the reaction.

☐ The rate of reaction of metals that react slowly at room temperature (or do not react) can be increased by passing oxygen over the hot metal.

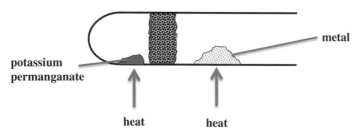

☐ The purpose of the potassium permanganate is to supply oxygen when heated (the –ate ending indicates that the compound contains oxygen).

☐ The 'fierceness' of the reaction between the metal and oxygen can be used to place metals in order of their reactivity (or activity).

☐ From the observations, the order of reactivity is found.

$$\textbf{LEAST REACTIVE} \quad \longrightarrow \quad \textbf{MOST REACTIVE}$$

e.g. **copper**   **lead**   **iron**   **zinc**   **aluminium**   **magnesium**

Reaction with water

☐ Lithium, sodium and potassium 'fizz' when added to water, showing that a gas is being given off 'in a hurry'; they catch fire and burn with a characteristic flame colour.

☐ From the observations, the order of reactivity is found.

LEAST REACTIVE ⟶ MOST REACTIVE

lithium   sodium   potassium

☐ With alkali metals, the rate of reaction with water increases going down the group; from this trend the reactivity of caesium and rubidium can be predicted.

LEAST REACTIVE ⟶ MOST REACTIVE

lithium   sodium   potassium   rubidium   caesium

☐ With calcium and magnesium, the rate is sufficiently slow for the gas to be collected; the gas can be identified to be hydrogen since it burns with a pop.

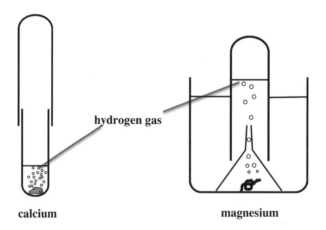

calcium   magnesium

☐ The products of the reaction of a metal with water will be the same whatever the metal and whatever the rate of the reaction, i.e. the gas produced in the reaction of lithium, sodium and potassium with water is hydrogen.

Reaction with dilute acids

☐ Some metals react quite vigorously with water, others relatively slowly; the rate of reaction of metals with dilute acids is even greater.

☐ The gas that is produced in the reaction is hydrogen.

☐ From the observations, the order of reactivity is found.

LEAST REACTIVE $\longrightarrow$ **MOST REACTIVE**

e.g. **copper   lead   iron   zinc   aluminium   magnesium**

☐ Copper does **not** react with dilute acid.

☐ When a metal reacts with a dilute acid, hydrogen gas is formed; the metal atoms lose electrons to become positive metal ions; the H^+ (aq) ions in the acid accept the electrons to form the gas.

$$2H^+(aq) \quad + \quad 2e^- \longrightarrow \quad H_2(g)$$

☐ A salt is the other product of the reaction.

ACID   +   METAL $\longrightarrow$ **SALT   +   HYDROGEN**

e.g.
aluminium + dilute sulphuric acid $\longrightarrow$ **aluminium sulphate + hydrogen**

☐ The electrons come from the metal atoms as the atoms lose electrons to form metal ions.

☐ This type of reaction is similar to a neutralisation reaction since the ions are 'cancelled out' and, as a result, the pH of the solution increases towards 7 as the reaction proceeds (see notes on page 64); however, the H^+ (aq) ions form hydrogen gas, **not** water.

$$2H^+(aq) \quad + \quad 2e^- \longrightarrow \quad H_2(g)$$

☐ The method used to prepare a salt is the same as that used with an insoluble metal oxide and insoluble metal carbonate with the excess metal being filtered off.

☐ Note that the reactions of dilute nitric acid with metals do **not** produce hydrogen gas.

Spectator ions: reactions of metals

- Spectator ions do not take part in chemical reactions; the ion equation shows the ions that are actually involved in the reaction.

- The idea of spectator ions can also be applied to reactions of metals with acid.

Example: The reaction of magnesium with dilute hydrochloric acid

$$Mg\,(s) \quad + \quad 2HCl\,(aq) \longrightarrow MgCl_2\,(aq) \quad + \quad H_2\,(g)$$

This equation can be rewritten to show the ions present.

$$Mg\,(s) + 2H^+\,(aq) \text{ and } 2Cl^-\,(aq) \longrightarrow Mg^{2+}\,(aq) \text{ and } 2Cl^-\,(aq) + H_2\,(g)$$

Since the chloride ion has not changed during the reaction, it is a spectator ion and can be cancelled out.

$$Mg\,(s) + 2H^+\,(aq) \text{ and } 2\cancel{Cl^-}\,(aq) \longrightarrow Mg^{2+}\,(aq) \text{ and } 2\cancel{Cl^-}\,(aq) + H_2\,(g)$$

This leaves an equation that describes what is actually happening during the reaction of a metal with a dilute acid.

$$Mg\,(s) \quad + \quad 2H^+\,(aq) \longrightarrow Mg^{2+}\,(aq) \quad + \quad H_2\,(g)$$

Metals from the Earth's crust

- Metals vary in their readiness to react with other substances.

- Silver and gold are very unreactive metals; as a result, these metals do not easily join up with other elements to form compounds ... so they are found uncombined in the ground.

- Silver and gold have been known since the early civilisations ... used for making jewellery.

- More reactive metals join up (easily) with other elements ... so they are found in the ground in the form of metal compounds (ores).

- Copper is not very reactive but more reactive than silver and gold; it is found as an ore but is also found uncombined.

Metals from metal oxides

☐ Compounds of the more reactive metals are (relatively) difficult to decompose (break up) ... they are said to be stable; compounds of the less reactive metals are (relatively) easy to decompose ... they are said to be unstable.

☐ The method of extraction of a metal is related to its reactivity.

☐ Only a few metal oxides decompose on heating alone to form the metal and oxygen gas,

  e.g. the oxides of silver, gold and mercury.

  metal oxide ⟶ metal + oxygen

☐ The gas can be identified as oxygen since it relights a glowing splint.

☐ Oxides of the more reactive metals do **not** break up on heating alone; other methods must be used to break up the oxides of these metals.

☐ Copper is more reactive than silver, gold and mercury and cannot be broken up by heating alone; however, it is a relatively unreactive metal and can be obtained from its ore by gentle heating with charcoal, a form of the element carbon.

☐ Iron and lead are other metals that can be obtained from their ores by heating with carbon.

☐ It is not possible to extract metals more reactive than iron by heating their ores with carbon; electricity, not discovered until the 18th century, has to be used instead (see notes on page 135).

The reactivity series

☐ The reactions of metals with oxygen, water and acid can be used to place metals in order of their 'readiness' to form compounds; this order of metals is known as the **reactivity series** with the most reactive metals at the top; the order is based on observations,

e.g.   speed of reaction; energy released.

☐ Metals high up in the reactivity series (relatively reactive metals) have a greater tendency to react quicker with more energy released than metals further down the reactivity series.

☐ Metals high up in the reactivity series form compounds that are relatively stable, i.e. going down the reactivity series, metals form compounds that are increasingly 'easy' to break up.

> **REACTIVE metals are likely to form STABLE COMPOUNDS.**
> **UNREACTIVE metals are likely to form UNSTABLE COMPOUNDS.**

☐ Hydrogen is included in the order; metals that react with dilute acid to produce hydrogen are place above hydrogen in the series; metals that do not react are placed below hydrogen.

As elements: most reactive metals at the top				As compounds: least reactive compounds at top
metal	with oxygen	with water	with acid	as oxides
potassium sodium lithium calcium magnesium aluminium zinc iron nickel tin lead *hydrogen* copper mercury silver gold	metals that are stored under oil	metals that react with cold water	metals that are too reactive to try in acid	metal oxides do not decompose on heating with carbon; electrical energy required to decompose compounds
			metals that react to form hydrogen	metal oxides decompose on heating with carbon
			metals that do not react with dilute acids	metal oxides decompose on heating to form metal

The electrochemical series

☐ When a metal element reacts to form a compound, the metal atoms lose electrons to form positive ions.

$e.g.$

$$Na \longrightarrow Na^+ + e^-$$
$$Mg \longrightarrow Mg^{2+} + 2e^-$$
$$Al \longrightarrow Al^{3+} + 3e^-$$

☐ The metal elements (atoms) can be placed in order of their measured ability to lose electrons to form metal ions; this order is called the **electrochemical series**.

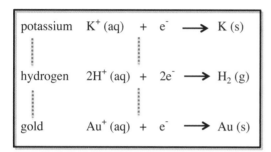

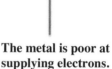

The metal is good at supplying electrons.

The metal is poor at supplying electrons.

☐ The Data Booklet, page 7, shows the position of some metals in the electrochemical series.

☐ The metals are listed in the form of ion-electron equations in which metal ions (in solution) gain electrons to form metal atoms (reduction reactions).

☐ Metals high up in the electrochemical series are 'good' at losing electrons; this means that the reaction is likely to go in the opposite direction from the way it is written in the Data Booklet,

e.g. potassium is likely to react:

element (atoms)   **compound (ions)**

$$K(s) \longrightarrow K^+ (aq) + e^-$$

☐ Metals low down in the electrochemical series are 'poor' at supplying electrons; this means that the metal ions are 'good' at gaining electrons and the reaction is likely to go in the same direction as the way it is written in the Data Booklet,

e.g. gold is likely to react:

compound (ions)   **element (atoms)**

$$Au^+ (aq) + e^- \longrightarrow Au(s)$$

☐ Hydrogen is included in the electrochemical series; metals above hydrogen in the series react with dilute acids; the metal atoms lose electrons that are accepted by the hydrogen ions, H^+ (aq) in the acids to produce hydrogen gas.

$$2H^+ \text{(aq)} \quad + \quad 2e^- \quad \longrightarrow \quad H_2 \text{(g)}$$

☐ Metals below hydrogen in the electrochemical series do **not** react with dilute acids.

☐ The order of metals in the electrochemical series is similar to (but not identical with) the order of metals in the reactivity series; this arises because he reactivity series is dependent on observations related to variable reaction conditions whereas the electrochemical series is based on measurements done under specific conditions.

3 Oxidation and reduction

Loss and gain of electrons

☐ When magnesium burns to form magnesium oxide, the metal atoms lose electrons to form positive metal ions in the compound.

$$Mg \longrightarrow Mg^{2+} + 2e^-$$

☐ Since the metal atoms are reacting with oxygen, this type of reaction was given the name **oxidation**; now, any reaction that involves the loss of electrons is referred to as oxidation.

☐ Every oxidation reaction must be accompanied by a reverse reaction in which electrons are gained; the reverse reaction is given the name **reduction**.

OIL	Oxidation	Is	Loss of electrons
RIG	Reduction	Is	Gain of electrons

Example: The reaction of magnesium with copper(II) ions, Cu^{2+} (aq)

Magnesium atoms lose electrons to form positive metal ions; this is an example of oxidation.

$$Mg \, (s) \longrightarrow Mg^{2+} (aq) + 2e^- \quad \textbf{oxidation}$$

Positive copper ions gain electrons to form copper atoms; this is an example of reduction.

$$Cu^{2+} (aq) + 2e^- \longrightarrow Cu \, (s) \quad \textbf{reduction}$$

☐ Equations that show the loss and gain of electrons are known as **ion-electron equations**; oxidation and reduction reactions are written as ion-electron equations; some ion-electron equations are found on page 7 of the Data Booklet.

☐ Reduction reactions are always copied as written in the Data Booklet; the ion-electron equation must be turned round for the oxidation reaction.

☐ Non-metal elements can also be involved in oxidation and reduction reactions.

Example: The reaction between bromine solution and iodide ions, $2I^-$ (aq)

Negative iodide ions lose electrons to form non-metal atoms (that join to form molecules); this is an example of oxidation.

$$2I^- \text{ (aq)} \longrightarrow I_2 \text{ (aq)} \quad + \quad 2e^- \qquad \textbf{oxidation}$$

Bromine atoms (in molecules) gain electrons to form negative bromide ions; this is an example of reduction.

$$Br_2 \text{ (aq)} \quad + \quad 2e^- \longrightarrow 2Br^- \text{ (aq)} \quad \textbf{reduction}$$

☐ Some ion-electron equations involve ions losing or gaining electrons to form other ions,

e.g. the reduction of iron(III) ions to iron(II) ions.

$$Fe^{3+} \text{ (aq)} \quad + \quad e^- \longrightarrow Fe^{2+} \text{ (aq)} \quad \textbf{reduction}$$

Redox reactions

☐ The ion-electron equations for the oxidation and reduction reactions can be combined to form the overall equation for the **redox reaction**.

☐ Redox reactions involve the transfer of electrons from one atom, molecule or ion to another.

☐ Care must be taken to ensure that the number of electrons in the oxidation cancels out with the number of electrons in the reduction.

Example 1: The reaction of magnesium with copper(II) sulphate solution

| **oxidation** | $Mg \text{ (s)}$ | $\longrightarrow$ | $Mg^{2+} \text{ (aq)}$ | $+$ | $2e^-$ |

| **reduction** | $Cu^{2+} \text{ (aq)}$ | $+$ | $2e^-$ | $\longrightarrow$ | $Cu \text{ (s)}$ |

redox reaction

$$Mg \text{ (s)} \quad + \quad Cu^{2+} \text{ (aq)} \longrightarrow Mg^{2+} \text{ (aq)} \quad + \quad Cu \text{ (s)}$$

Example 2:   The reaction of aluminium with dilute hydrochloric acid

| oxidation | $Al\,(s)$ | $\longrightarrow$ | $Al^{3+}\,(aq)$ | $+$ | $3e^-$ |

| reduction | $2H^+\,(aq)$ | $+$ | $2e^-$ | $\longrightarrow$ | $H_2\,(s)$ |

To cancel out the electrons, the oxidation must be multiplied by 2, and the reduction by 3.

oxidation $2Al\,(s)$ $\qquad\qquad\qquad\qquad$ $2Al^{3+}\,(aq)$ $+$ $6e^-$

reduction $6H^+\,(aq)$ $\quad+\quad 6e^-$ $\longrightarrow$ $3H_2\,(s)$

redox reaction $2Al\,(s)$ $\quad+\quad 6H^+\,(aq)$ $\longrightarrow$ $2Al^{3+}\,(aq)$ $+$ $3H_2\,(s)$

☐   The oxidation and reduction ion-electron equations can be written from the equation for the redox reaction.

Example 1:   The reaction of zinc with nickel(II) chloride solution

redox reaction $Zn\,(s)$ $+$ $Ni^{2+}\,(aq)$ $\longrightarrow$ $Zn^{2+}\,(aq)$ $+$ $Ni\,(s)$

oxidation $Zn\,(s)$ $\qquad\qquad\qquad$ $\longrightarrow$ $Zn^{2+}\,(aq)$ $+$ $2e^-$

reduction $Ni^{2+}\,(aq)$ $\quad+\quad 2e^-$ $\longrightarrow$ $Ni\,(s)$

Example 2:   The reaction of chlorine with sodium bromide solution

redox reaction $Cl_2\,(aq)$ $+$ $2Br^-\,(aq)$ $\longrightarrow$ $Br_2\,(aq)$ $+$ $2Cl^-\,(aq)$

oxidation $2Br^-\,(aq)$ $\qquad\qquad\qquad$ $\longrightarrow$ $Br_2\,(aq)$ $+$ $2e^-$

reduction $Cl_2\,(aq)$ $\quad+\quad 2e^-$ $\longrightarrow$ $2Cl^-\,(aq)$

Displacement reactions

☐ In the metal element there are metal atoms; in metal compounds there are positive metal ions.

☐ Metals high up in the electrochemical series are likely to react to form ions of the metal:

element (atoms)   **compound (ions)**

e.g. M_{high} (s) $\longrightarrow$ M^+_{high} (aq)   + e^-

This is an **oxidation** reaction.

☐ Ions of metals low down in the electrochemical series are likely to react to form the metal:

compound (ions)   **element (atoms)**

e.g. M^+_{low} (aq)   + e^- $\longrightarrow$ M_{low} (s)

This is a **reduction** reaction.

☐ When a metal higher up in the electrochemical series is added to a solution containing ions of a metal lower down in the electrochemical series, there is a chemical reaction as a result of a transfer of electrons from the atoms to the ions.

Example: Zinc is added to a solution of silver ions, Ag^+ (aq).

$$Zn\ (s) \quad\quad\quad \longrightarrow \quad Zn^{2+}\ (aq) \quad + \quad 2e^- \quad \textbf{oxidation}$$

$$2Ag^+\ (aq) \quad + \quad 2e^- \longrightarrow \ 2Ag\ (s) \quad\quad\quad \textbf{reduction}$$

$$Zn\ (s) \quad + \ 2Ag^+\ (aq) \quad \longrightarrow \quad Zn^{2+}\ (aq) \quad + \quad 2Ag\ (s) \quad \textbf{redox reaction}$$

☐ This kind of reaction is known as a **displacement reaction;** the metal lower down in the electrochemical series is displaced by the metal higher up,

e.g. zinc displaces silver (ions) from silver nitrate solution.

☐ A displacement reaction does **not** take place when a metal lower down in the electrochemical series is added to a solution containing ions of a metal higher up in the electrochemical series,

e.g. if copper is added to a solution of a sodium ions there is no reaction.

4 Making electricity

Batteries

☐ An electrochemical cell (or just cell for short) is a
device that can make electricity from chemical
reactions; two or more cells joined together make a
battery (of cells); nowadays the two words are
interchangeable.

☐ A typical cell is made up of two different metals in an
electrolyte,

e.g. the lemon cell.

lemon cell

☐ When a battery is in use, chemical reactions at each of the positive and
negative electrode result in the flow of electrons (electricity).

☐ Batteries "run down" and many eventually have to be replaced; this is
because the chemicals that take part in the chemical reactions are used up.

☐ Some batteries are rechargeable and can be used again,

e.g. a nickel-cadmium battery.

☐ When the battery is on charge, the chemical reactants are regenerated using
electricity.

using a battery (making electricity)

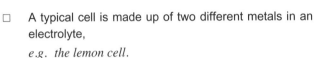

CHEMICAL REACTANTS ⇌ CHEMICAL PRODUCTS

recharging a battery (using electricity)

The magnesium/copper cell

☐ A metal higher up in the electrochemical series can displace a metal lower
down,

e.g. magnesium displaces copper (ions) from copper sulphate solution.

$Mg(s)$	$\longrightarrow$	$Mg^{2+}(aq)$ + $2e^-$		**oxidation**
$Cu^{2+}(aq)$ + $2e^-$	$\longrightarrow$	$Cu(s)$		**reduction**
$Mg(s)$ + $Cu^{2+}(aq)$	$\longrightarrow$	$Mg^{2+}(aq)$ + $Cu(s)$		**redox reaction**

☐ In a test tube reaction, the transfer of electrons cannot be put to use; however, in a cell the flow of electrons that results from the reactions can be used as a source of electricity.

☐ The magnesium/copper cell consists of two electrodes joined together by connecting wires; each electrode has a metal in a solution of the metal ions.

☐ A meter can be used to show the direction of electron flow.

☐ The two electrodes are also linked by means of a salt bridge; this is a piece of filter paper soaked in a salt solution; any salt solution that contains ions that do not react with the electrodes can be used,

e.g. a solution of potassium nitrate.

☐ the salt bridge provides ions that can move to complete the circuit.

☐ Magnesium is higher up than copper in the electrochemical series so there is a transfer of electrons through the meter from the magnesium atoms to the copper ions.

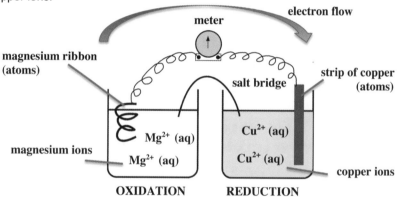

☐ Magnesium atoms from the metal lose electrons to form magnesium ions that go into solution.

$$Mg\,(s) \longrightarrow Mg^{2+}\,(aq) \;+\; 2e^- \qquad \textbf{oxidation}$$

The mass of the magnesium electrode decreases as a result.

☐ Copper ions in solution gain electrons to form copper atoms that appear as a solid.

$$Cu^{2+}\,(aq) \;+\; 2e^- \longrightarrow Cu\,(s) \qquad \textbf{reduction}$$

The mass of the copper electrode increases as a result.

Chemistry in Society

A flow of electrons

☐ The electrochemical series places metals in order of their ability to lose electrons to form positive ions; metals higher up are more likely to lose electrons than metals lower down,

e.g. magnesium is more likely to lose electrons than copper.

$$Mg\,(s) \longrightarrow Mg^{2+}\,(aq) + 2e^- \qquad \textbf{more likely}$$
$$Cu\,(s) \longrightarrow Cu^{2+}\,(aq) + 2e^- \qquad \textbf{less likely}$$

☐ When two metals are attached to each other, there is always a flow of electrons from the metal higher in the electrochemical series to the metal lower in the electrochemical series.

☐ Cells, with a meter in the circuit, can be set up to show the direction of electron flow; the electrons move through the connecting wires.

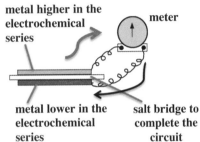

metal higher in the electrochemical series

meter

metal lower in the electrochemical series

salt bridge to complete the circuit

Voltages

☐ When two different metals are linked together with an electrolyte to complete the circuit, a voltage is produced due to the difference in the abilities of the metals to lose electrons.

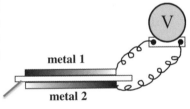

metal 1

metal 2

salt bridge to complete the circuit

☐ The arrangement of metals in the electrochemical series is from voltmeter readings.

☐ Different metal pairs produce different voltages; metals that are far apart in the electrochemical series produce higher voltages,

e.g. magnesium connected to silver will produce a higher voltage than iron connected to silver; lead connected to copper will produce a lower voltage than zinc connected to copper.

Non-metal electrodes

☐ A redox reaction results in reduction and oxidation, i.e. electron-gain and electron-loss; many redox reactions involve metals (atoms forming ions) and metal ions (metal ions forming atoms) but some do not,

e.g. the reaction between iron(III) ions, Fe^{3+} (aq), and iodide ions, $2I^-$ (aq), is a redox reaction.

oxidation $\quad 2I^-$ (aq) $\quad \longrightarrow \quad I_2$ (aq) $\quad + \quad 2\,e^-$

reduction $\quad Fe^{3+}$ (aq) $\quad + \quad e^- \longrightarrow \quad Fe^{2+}$ (aq)

☐ A cell can be set up with carbon electrodes ... the flow of electrons in the wires of the circuit indicates that a redox reaction is taking place.

☐ A salt bridge is again used to complete the circuit.

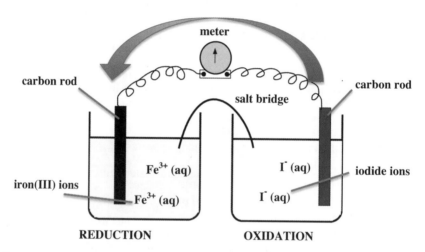

☐ The iodide ions lose electrons to form iodine molecules; the iodine can be detected using starch solution ... a blue/black colour shows that the presence of iodine.

$\quad 2I^-$ (aq) $\quad \longrightarrow \quad I_2$ (aq) $\quad + \quad 2\,e^- \quad$ **oxidation**

☐ The iron(III) ions gain electrons to form iron(II) ions; the iron(II) ions can be detected using ferroxyl indicator ... a blue colour shows the presence of iron(II) ions.

$\quad Fe^{3+}$ (aq) $\quad + \quad e^- \longrightarrow \quad Fe^{2+}$ (aq $\quad$ **reduction**

Fuel cells

☐ A battery is a device that generates electricity,
e.g. for lighting or turning a motor.

☐ A battery has all of its chemicals stored inside and when in use, these are being converted to products; a battery will eventually 'run down' and you either throw it away or recharge it.

☐ A **fuel cell** is also a device that makes electricity; with a fuel cell, as long as there is a flow of reactants into the cell, the electricity flows out of the cell.

☐ Every fuel cell has two electrodes, one positive and one negative; the reactions that produce electricity take place at the electrodes and their rate is increased by the presence of suitable catalysts.

☐ Every fuel cell also has an electrolyte that allows ions to move from one electrode to the other.

☐ Hydrogen is the most common fuel and the other reactant is usually oxygen.

The hydrogen/oxygen fuel cell

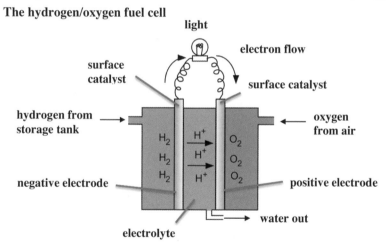

☐ At the negative electrode of the cell the hydrogen molecules dissociate to form atoms on the catalyst surface.

$$H_2 \longrightarrow 2H$$

☐ Oxidation of the hydrogen atoms result in the formation of positively charged hydrogen ions and negatively charged electrons.

$$\text{oxidation} \qquad 2H \longrightarrow 2H^+ + 2e^-$$

☐ The freed electrons travel through a wire creating the electric current.

☐ The ions travel through the electrolyte to the positive electrode of the cell; on reaching the positive electrode, the hydrogen ions are reunited with the electrons and the two react with oxygen to produce water.

$$\text{reduction} \qquad 4H^+ + O_2 + 4e^- \longrightarrow 2H_2O$$

☐ One great appeal of the hydrogen/oxygen fuel cell is that electricity is generated with very little pollution since the product of the two reactions is water.

$$2H_2 \longrightarrow 4H^+ + 4e^-$$

$$4H^+ + O_2 + 4e^- \longrightarrow 2H_2O$$

$$\overline{}$$

$$2H_2 + O_2 \longrightarrow 2H_2O$$

$$\overline{}$$

5 Using electricity

Extraction of metals

☐ Reactive metals are always found as positive ions in metal compounds; these metal elements cannot be obtained by heating their oxides with carbon … they can only be obtained by using electrical energy to break up their molten compounds.

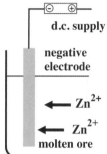

☐ The process used to extract the more reactive metals from their ores is an example of **electrolysis**.

d.c. supply

negative electrode

☐ Since metal ions have a positive charge, they are attracted to the negative electrode where they gain electrons to form the metal as the element.

$\longleftarrow Zn^{2+}$

e.g. $Zn^{2+} + 2e^- \longrightarrow Zn$ **reduction**

$\longleftarrow Zn^{2+}$

molten ore

Extraction of aluminium

☐ The extraction of aluminium is another example of **electrolysis**.

☐ Because it is a reactive metal, electrical energy is required to extract aluminium from its ore; since electrical energy is required in the extraction process, the plants are (usually) sited near cheap sources of electricity.

☐ Electricity is passed through a molten mixture containing aluminium oxide.

☐ Both the positive and negative electrodes are made of carbon.

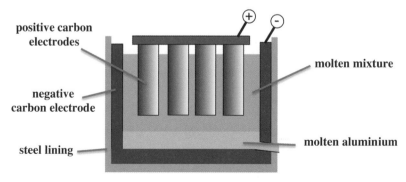

positive carbon electrodes

molten mixture

negative carbon electrode

molten aluminium

steel lining

☐ At the negative electrode, positive aluminium ions gain electrons to form aluminium.

$$Al^{3+} + 3e^- \longrightarrow Al \qquad \textbf{reduction}$$

☐ The molten aluminium sinks to the bottom of the tank and can be removed.

☐ At the positive electrode, carbon reacts with the oxygen formed to produce carbon dioxide and so the electrodes have to be replaced at regular intervals.

Electroplating

☐ During electroplating one metal is coated with a thin layer of another metal; the process can give a very attractive surface-coating to the metal underneath.

☐ Electroplating is another example of **electrolysis**.

☐ The metal that is to be coated is made the negative electrode of a cell; the ions of the plating metal are in the electrolyte.

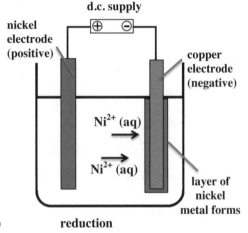

☐ In the nickel electroplating of copper, copper is made the negative electrode and the electrolyte contains positive nickel ions, Ni^{2+} (aq).

☐ During the process, the positive nickel ions are attracted to the negative copper electrode where they gain electrons to form a layer of nickel atoms.

$$Ni^{2+} + 2e^- \longrightarrow Ni \text{ (s)} \qquad \textbf{reduction}$$

☐ At the positive electrode, nickel atoms form nickel ions, Ni^{2+} (aq).

$$Ni \text{ (s)} \longrightarrow Ni^{2+} \text{(aq)} + 2e^- \qquad \textbf{oxidation}$$

☐ The overall result of this electrolysis is that the positive electrode (nickel) decreases in mass and the negative electrode (copper) increases in mass; nickel metal is transferred from the positive electrode to the negative electrode.

Chemistry in Society

Purifying copper

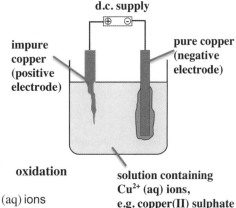

☐ Pure copper can be obtained from impure copper by **electrolysis**.

☐ At the impure copper electrode, the electrode 'disappears' as the copper atoms form Cu^{2+} (aq) ions and the impurities fall to the bottom of the cell.

d.c. supply

impure copper (positive electrode)

pure copper (negative electrode)

solution containing Cu^{2+} (aq) ions, e.g. copper(II) sulphate solution

$$Cu \ (s) \longrightarrow Cu^{2+}(aq) + 2e^- \quad \textbf{oxidation}$$

☐ At the pure copper electrode, Cu^{2+} (aq) ions gain electrons to form copper atoms.

$$Cu^{2+} + 2e^- \longrightarrow Cu \ (s) \quad \textbf{reduction}$$

☐ The overall result of this electrolysis is that the positive electrode (impure copper) decreases in mass and the negative electrode (pure copper) increases in mass; copper metal is transferred from the impure electrode to the pure electrode.

Anodising

☐ Aluminium is a reactive metal and yet does not seem to corrode as quickly as expected; this is because aluminium reacts with the oxygen of the air to form a thin protective layer of aluminium oxide.

☐ **Anodising** involves increasing the thickness of the oxide layer of aluminium.

☐ Aluminium is made the positive electrode (called the anode), hence the name of the process.

☐ The oxide coating from anodising is a better protector of the metal than its normal oxide coating and anodised aluminium is used to make parts of doors, window frames, boats, planes and sports equipment; it can also be coloured using dyes, making it more attractive.

- Anodising is an example of **electrolysis**.

- The electrolysis of dilute sulphuric acid results in the discharge of oxygen at the positive electrode; during this discharge, oxygen can react with aluminium metal of the electrode.

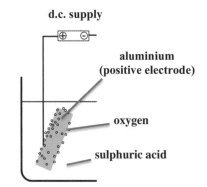

d.c. supply

aluminium
(positive electrode)

oxygen

sulphuric acid

A question of opposites

(a) Making electricity

- In a battery (cell), chemical reactions are used to produce a d.c. (direct current) supply of electricity.

- Electrons are lost to the circuit at the negative electrode of the battery due to an oxidation reaction; electrons are gained from the circuit at the positive electrode of the battery due to a reduction reaction.

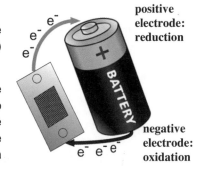

positive electrode: reduction

negative electrode: oxidation

(b) Using electricity

- The reverse is true in the process of electrolysis … electricity is used to make chemical reactions take place.

- During electrolysis, there is a surplus of electrons at the negative electrode and a deficit of electrons at the positive electrode.

- At the negative electrode, electrons are gained from the circuit; this is reduction.

- At the positive electrode, electrons are lost to the circuit; this is oxidation.

Example: Electrolysis of copper(II) chloride solution

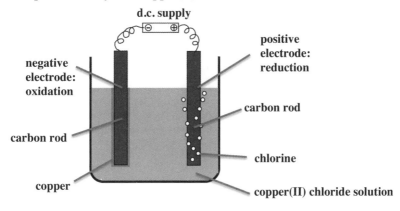

d.c. supply

negative electrode: oxidation

positive electrode: reduction

carbon rod

carbon rod

chlorine

copper

copper(II) chloride solution

☐ In the electrolysis of copper(II) chloride solution, the copper ions are attracted to the negative electrode where electrons are gained from the carbon electrode to form copper metal.

$$Cu^{2+}(aq) + 2e^- \longrightarrow Cu(s) \quad \textbf{reduction}$$

☐ The chloride ions are attracted to the positive electrode where electrons are lost to form chlorine gas.

$$2Cl^-(aq) \longrightarrow Cl_2(g) + 2e^- \quad \textbf{oxidation}$$

(c) A rechargeable battery

☐ When a rechargeable battery is being used to make electricity, it is like any other battery ... an oxidation reaction provides electrons at the negative electrode and a reduction reaction accepts electrons at the positive electrode.

negative electrode: $X \longrightarrow X^+ + e^- \quad$ oxidation

in use

positive electrode: $Y^+ + e^- \longrightarrow Y \quad$ reduction

☐ However, when it is being charged, electricity is being used to reverse the chemical reactions in order to regenerate the reactants; electrolysis is taking place.

negative electrode: $X^+ + e^- \longrightarrow X \quad$ reduction

on charge

positive electrode: $Y \longrightarrow Y^+ + e^- \quad$ oxidation

6 Corrosion

An unwanted reaction

☐ Our modern world depends on metals; however, there is one big problem with metals ... when some are left in the open air, the metal breaks up.

☐ This is because there is a chemical reaction at the surface of the metal ... the atoms react to form a compound that can flake off, exposing fresh metal; this process is called **corrosion** and in the special case of iron, it is called **rusting**.

☐ Some metals corrode easily,

e.g. iron.

☐ Others hardly corrode at all,

e.g. silver and gold.

☐ Rust is not an element; when iron rusts, the iron atoms lose two electrons, forming iron(II) ions, $Fe^{2+}(aq)$.

$$Fe(s) \longrightarrow Fe^{2+}(aq) + 2e^- \qquad \textbf{oxidation}$$

... so rust is an ionic compound.

☐ Corrosion of any metal involves the metal atoms losing electrons to form ions,

e.g. magnesium ions are formed when magnesium corrodes.

$$Mg(s) \longrightarrow Mg^{2+}(aq) + 2e^- \qquad \textbf{oxidation}$$

What is required for rusting?

☐ When iron rusts, the metal atoms react to form a compound; the metal gradually 'disappears' as the surface breaks up.

☐ The conditions that cause rusting can be found by setting up test tubes in which iron nails are exposed to different conditions and then examined to find out which nails have rusted.

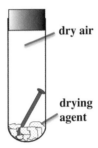

dry air

drying agent

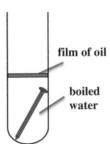

film of oil

boiled water

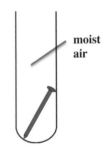

moist air

iron in a test-tube of air; moisture of the air removed by a drying agent

iron immersed in water which has been boiled to drive out any dissolved air, then covered with a film of oil to prevent any air re-dissolving

iron in a moist-air atmosphere

NO RUSTING   **NO RUSTING**   **RUSTING**

☐ Water and oxygen (air) are required for the corrosion of any metal.

☐ The electrons lost by the metal atoms are accepted by the water and oxygen.

$$2H_2O \, (l) \quad + \quad O_2 \, (g) \quad + \quad 4e^- \quad \longrightarrow \quad 4OH^- \, (aq) \qquad \textbf{reduction}$$

A rusting indicator

☐ When iron rusts, the iron atoms lose two electrons, forming iron(II) ions, Fe^{2+} (aq).

☐ Ferroxyl indicator is a solution that can be used to show that rusting is taking place; this indicator reacts with iron(II) ions, Fe^{2+} (aq), to form a distinctive blue colour.

The effect of salt and acid

☐ The intensity of the blue colour can be used to give an idea of the extent of rusting.

☐ A gel to which ferroxyl indicator has been added can be used to find the effect of salt (sodium chloride) solution and acid on the rate of rusting; by putting iron nails in a gel, the product of any rusting is held at the site of the reaction around each nail.

iron nail in a ferroxyl gel

iron nail in a ferroxyl gel to which salt has been added

iron nail in a ferroxyl gel to which acid has been added

☐ Both salt and acid increase the rate of rusting; the solutions contain ions and conduct electricity; the rusting of iron involves ions and electrons; therefore rusting takes place more easily in the presence of ionic solutions.

☐ Since covalent compounds are made up of neutral molecules, they do not have any effect on the rate of rusting,

e.g. glucose, $C_6H_{12}O_6$.

☐ In addition, the ion that gives the characteristic properties to an acidic solution is the $H^+(aq)$ ion; since iron is above hydrogen in the electrochemical series, a displacement reaction can occur between the iron atoms in the metal and the $H^+(aq)$ ions.

$$Fe\,(s) \longrightarrow Fe^{2+}(aq) + 2e^- \qquad \textbf{oxidation}$$

$$2H^+\,(aq) + 2e^- \longrightarrow H_2\,(g) \qquad \textbf{reduction}$$

The effect of other metals

☐ The electrochemical series places metals in order of their ability to lose electrons to form positive ions; when two metals are attached to each other, there is always a flow of electrons from the metal higher in the electrochemical series to the metal lower in the electrochemical series.

☐ A gel containing ferroxyl indicator can be used to show the effect of attaching magnesium and copper to different iron nails.

experiment A

**iron nail alone
in a ferroxyl gel**

experiment B

**copper attached
to iron nail
in a ferroxyl gel**

experiment C

**magnesium attached
to iron nail
in a ferroxyl gel**

☐ The intensity of the blue colour in experiment **B** is greater than in experiment **A**; attaching copper to the iron nail increases the rate of rusting.

☐ There is no sign of a blue colour in experiment **C**; the iron nail with magnesium attached to it does **not** rust.

Electrochemical protection: attaching to scrap magnesium

☐ Rusting can be prevented by attaching iron to a metal that is higher up in the electrochemical series; electrons flow from the metal to the iron; this method of preventing rusting is known as **electrochemical protection**.

☐ Scrap magnesium, a relatively cheap source of the metal, can be used, *e.g. underground pipes made of iron are protected using scrap magnesium.*

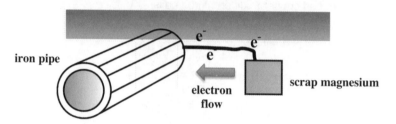

☐ Magnesium has a great ability to lose electrons:

$$Mg\,(s) \longrightarrow Mg^{2+}\,(aq) + 2e^- \qquad \textbf{oxidation}$$

☐ Electrons flow from the magnesium to the iron as the magnesium corrodes; this helps to prevent the iron atoms losing electrons.

$$Fe\,(s) \longrightarrow Fe^{2+}\,(aq) + 2e^-$$

electrons from the scrap magnesium help to prevent rusting

☐ Since lumps of magnesium are sacrificed to protect the iron, this method of stopping rusting is also called **sacrificial protection**; from time to time, new pieces of magnesium must be attached to the iron to replace the corroded scrap.

☐ Scrap zinc can also be used for sacrificial protection.

Electrochemical protection:
attaching to the negative terminal of a battery

☐ The rusting of iron is considerably reduced by attaching the metal to the negative terminal of a battery,

e.g. the bodywork of a car is usually attached to the negative terminal of the battery to help to slow down rusting.

☐ This is another example of **electrochemical protection.**

☐ The chemical reaction at the negative terminal of a battery produces electrons; electrons flow from the battery to the iron.

☐ As with sacrificial protection the flow of electrons helps to prevent the iron atoms from losing electrons.

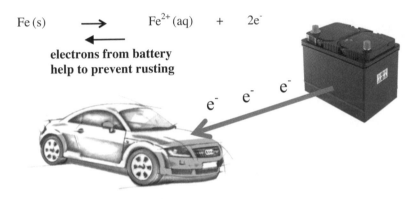

$$Fe\,(s) \longrightarrow Fe^{2+}(aq) + 2e^-$$

**electrons from battery
help to prevent rusting**

Physical protection of iron

☐ The process of rusting requires water and oxygen; one way to prevent rusting is to keep water and oxygen away from the metal.

☐ There are different ways of providing a surface barrier, i.e. providing **physical protection** of iron.

(a) Painting, greasing and oiling

☐ This is a very common method of trying to prevent rusting; it is essential to keep the paint in good condition since rusting results when the paintwork is not properly maintained.

(b) Coating with plastic

☐ Iron or steel can be coated with plastic to prevent rusting.

(c) Electroplating

☐ The iron or steel is coated with a thin layer of another metal, *e.g. chromium, silver or gold.*

(d) Tin plating

☐ This is a special form of electroplating; unfortunately, if the surface layer of tin is broken and the iron becomes exposed, the iron will rust faster as a result of the contact with the less reactive tin.

(e) Galvanising

☐ A thin surface coat of zinc is put on an object by dipping the object in molten zinc; if the surface coat of zinc is broken, the iron still does not rust; the more reactive zinc continues to sacrificially protect the iron.

A bit more about corrosion

☐ When iron rusts, metal atoms change to metal ions.

$$Fe\,(s) \longrightarrow Fe^{2+}(aq) + 2e^{-} \qquad \textbf{oxidation}$$

☐ Water and oxygen are required for corrosion to take place; the electrons lost by the metal atoms are accepted by the water and oxygen; this is an example of a reduction reaction.

$$2H_2O\,(l) + O_2\,(g) + 4e^{-} \longrightarrow 4OH^{-}(aq) \qquad \textbf{reduction}$$

☐ Ferroxyl indicator is a solution that will react with both the oxidation product of rusting and the reduction product of corrosion, i.e. iron(II) ions, Fe^{2+} (aq), and hydroxide ions, OH^{-}(aq), respectively.

☐ A colour change is associated with each of the reactions.

Reaction	Product	Colour observed
oxidation (of iron)	Fe^{2+} (aq) ions	blue
reduction	OH^{-} (aq) ions	pink

□ Ferroxyl indicator can be used to find out about the reactions taking place in cells involving iron nails; a blue colour shows the presence of iron(II) ions, Fe^{2+} (aq), (oxidation of iron) and a pink colour shows the presence of OH^-(aq) ions (reduction).

□ The purpose of the electrolyte is to complete the circuit; a solution of any ionic compound can be used, as long as the ions do not react with the electrodes.

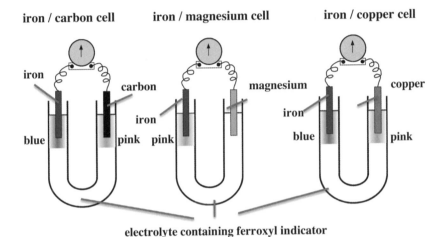

iron / carbon cell   **iron / magnesium cell**   **iron / copper cell**

electrolyte containing ferroxyl indicator

(a) The iron/carbon cell

□ The blue colour around the iron shows Fe^{2+} (aq) ions to be present.
The reaction taking place is:

$$Fe(s) \longrightarrow Fe^{2+}(aq) + 2e^- \qquad \textbf{oxidation}$$

□ The pink colour around the carbon shows OH^- (aq) ions to be present.
The reaction taking place is:

$$2H_2O(l) + O_2(g) + 4e^- \longrightarrow 4OH^-(aq) \quad \textbf{reduction}$$

□ Electrons flow from the iron to the carbon.

(b) The iron/magnesium cell

☐ Electrons flow from the magnesium to the iron because magnesium is above iron in the electrochemical series.

☐ The pink colour around the iron shows OH⁻ (aq) ions to be present.
The reaction taking place is:

$$2H_2O \text{ (l)} \quad + \quad O_2 \text{ (g)} \quad + \quad 4e^- \longrightarrow \quad 4OH^- \text{ (aq)} \qquad \textbf{reduction}$$

(c) The iron/copper cell

☐ Electrons flow from the iron to the copper because iron is above copper in the electrochemical series.

☐ The blue colour around the iron shows Fe^{2+} (aq) ions to be present.
The reaction taking place is:

$$Fe \text{ (s)} \longrightarrow \quad Fe^{2+} \text{ (aq)} \quad + \quad 2e^- \qquad \textbf{oxidation}$$

☐ The pink colour around the copper shows OH⁻ (aq) ions to be present.
The reaction taking place is:

$$2H_2O \text{ (l)} \quad + \quad O_2 \text{ (g)} \quad + \quad 4e^- \longrightarrow \quad 4OH^- \text{ (aq)} \qquad \textbf{reduction}$$

7 Plastics

Useful materials ***

☐ Plastics are a family of materials that can be moulded when soft and then set into shape.

☐ Plastics are not natural ... they are examples of **synthetic** materials, i.e. made by the chemical industry; most plastics are made from chemicals obtained from oil.

☐ Most plastics are non-conductors of electricity and poor conductors of heat; they are relatively light and insoluble in water; as a result of their properties, they are now used to replace a variety of natural materials,

  e.g. plastic tea-spoons can replace metal tea-spoons since they are light and poor conductors of heat.

☐ Most plastics are relatively cheap to produce ... this is another reason that they are used to make disposable items,

  e.g. plastic cutlery and cups.

Problems with plastics ***

☐ Plastics are quite cheap, light and can be easily moulded into any shape; however, plastics can also be a problem.

☐ The leaves from the trees are **biodegradable** ('bio' refers to living things and 'degradable' means 'able to rot away'); leaves are broken down by bacteria (living organisms) and weather and eventually decompose.

☐ Plastics are **not** biodegradable and can cause unsightly litter as well as being a danger to animals looking for food.

☐ Fires involving plastics are extremely dangerous and can lead to further pollution problems; poisonous fumes can be produced when they are burning.

☐ Since polymers have carbon atoms in the chains, carbon monoxide, CO, can be given off from just about any burning plastic.

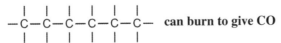

☐ Other gases produced include hydrogen chloride, HCl (g), from poly(chloroethene) and hydrogen cyanide, HCN (g), from polyurethane.

poly(chloroethene)
$$-\overset{\displaystyle |}{\underset{\displaystyle |}{C}}-\overset{\displaystyle |}{\underset{\displaystyle |}{C}}-\overset{\displaystyle |}{\underset{\displaystyle |}{C}}-\overset{\displaystyle |}{\underset{\displaystyle |}{C}}-\overset{\displaystyle |}{\underset{\displaystyle |}{C}}-\overset{\displaystyle |}{\underset{\displaystyle |}{C}}-$$
CI   CI   CI   **can burn to give HCl**

polyurethane
$$-\overset{\displaystyle |}{\underset{\displaystyle |}{C}}-\overset{\displaystyle |}{\underset{\displaystyle |}{C}}-\overset{\displaystyle |}{\underset{\displaystyle |}{C}}-\overset{\displaystyle |}{\underset{\displaystyle |}{C}}-\overset{\displaystyle |}{\underset{\displaystyle |}{C}}-\overset{\displaystyle |}{\underset{\displaystyle |}{C}}-$$
CN   CN   CN   **can burn to give HCN**

☐ The gases produced depend on the elements in the plastic.

Ceramic materials ***

☐ The early ceramic materials (ceramics) include porcelain, used to make decorative items and objects of fine art,

   e.g. vases, plates and tiles.

☐ Ceramic materials display a wide range of properties that offer many advantages compared to other materials,

   e.g. in general, they are hard (wear resistant), resistant to corrosion and high temperatures and most are poor/non-conductors of heat and electricity.

☐ This leads to their modern use in a wide variety of domestic, industrial and building products.

Disposal of plastics ***

☐ Our use of plastics has grown at a tremendous rate over the last 20 to 30 years with an ever-increasing variety of products; however, the vast majority of plastics are quickly discarded.

☐ Most unwanted plastics are **buried in land-fill sites**; while this is a relatively cheap and effective way of removal, there are no other benefits; also, plastics tend to be light and bulky as well as non-biodegradable and so will sit in the sites for many years.

☐ Some plastics are **burned in an incinerator** and the energy released can be put to use; however, the burning of plastics produces carbon dioxide gas, and increasing levels of this gas in the atmosphere may be contributing to global warming.

☐ Most plastics are made from chemicals that come from oil so **recycling** makes good use of a non-renewable resource; with recycling, waste plastic is reprocessed into useful products, sometimes completely different in form from the original,

e.g. *melting down soft drink bottles and then casting them as plastic chairs and tables.*

☐ However, difficulties with sorting plastics can mean that the range of new products is limited; indeed, it would appear that in many instances strategies for recycling are not economically viable compared to first-time processing.

Effect of heat ***

☐ Plastics can be classified according to what happens to them on heating.

☐ **Thermoplastics** (thermosoftening plastics) soften on heating; this enables them to be reshaped over and over again,

e.g. *poly(ethene) (or polythene) is used to make plastic bottles.*

☐ **Thermosetting** plastics harden on heating and do not melt on reheating; thermosetting plastics have quite different uses from thermoplastics,

e.g. *melamine formaldehyde is used to make Formica and laminate flooring; urea formaldehyde is used in laminates, textiles, adhesive resins, etc.*

New materials ***

☐ New materials are constantly being developed with special and unique properties to meet the demands of society,

e.g. *Kevlar and poly(ethenol).*

☐ Kevlar is used to make bullet-proof vests as it is very strong.

- Poly(ethenol) is soluble in water and is used to make:
  - * disposable laundry bags for hospitals ... the bags dissolve in water and so the dirty linen is released without being handled by hospital workers, reducing the risk of infection;
  - * surgical stitches ... the thread dissolves in water over time and does not need to be removed;
  - * protective coatings for new cars can be made of poly(ethenol) ... the dissolving polymer can be hosed off with warm water.

- Plastics that biodegrade have also been made.

Very large molecules

- The molecules in plastics are made by the joining up of lots of small molecules called **monomers** ('mono' meaning one or a single unit) to make very long chains, often consisting of thousands of atoms linked together.

- The plastics formed are called **polymers** ('poly' meaning many) and the process used to make them is known as **polymerisation**.

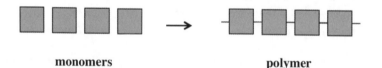

monomers   **polymer**

- Many polymers have only carbon atoms in the actual chain.

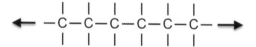

chain keeps going at both ends

- The name of the polymer comes from the name of the monomer,
  e.g. poly(ethene) is made from ethene.

Addition polymers

☐ Many of the monomers are small unsaturated molecules, i.e. small molecules with a carbon to carbon double covalent bond.

☐ The monomer molecules join together by the opening of the carbon to carbon double bonds to give a long chain of carbon to carbon single covalent bonds. *e.g.*

$$\underset{\textbf{ethene}}{\begin{array}{c} H\ \ H \\ |\ \ \ | \\ C=C \\ |\ \ \ | \\ H\ \ H \end{array}} + \begin{array}{c} H\ \ H \\ |\ \ \ | \\ C=C \\ |\ \ \ | \\ H\ \ H \end{array} + \begin{array}{c} H\ \ H \\ |\ \ \ | \\ C=C \\ |\ \ \ | \\ H\ \ H \end{array} \longrightarrow \underset{\textbf{poly(ethene)}}{\begin{array}{c} H\ \ H\ \ H\ \ H\ \ H\ \ H \\ |\ \ \ |\ \ \ |\ \ \ |\ \ \ |\ \ \ | \\ -C-C-C-C-C-C- \\ |\ \ \ |\ \ \ |\ \ \ |\ \ \ |\ \ \ | \\ H\ \ H\ \ H\ \ H\ \ H\ \ H \end{array}}$$

☐ Polymers formed in this way are called **addition polymers** and the process is named **addition polymerisation**.

☐ Addition polymers have a two carbon repeating unit; this is based on the two carbon atoms originally joined by the double bond.

$$\begin{array}{c} H\ \ H \\ |\ \ \ | \\ C=C \\ |\ \ \ | \\ H\ \ H \end{array} \longrightarrow \underset{\textbf{repeating unit}}{\boxed{\begin{array}{c} |\ \ \ | \\ C-C \\ |\ \ \ | \end{array}} \begin{array}{c} |\ \ \ |\ \ \ |\ \ \ | \\ C-C-C-C- \\ |\ \ \ |\ \ \ |\ \ \ | \end{array}}$$

☐ The monomer can be identified from the two carbon repeating unit in the polymer and forming a double bond. *e.g.*

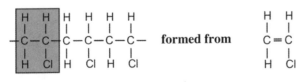

poly(chloroethene)   formed from   chloroethene

☐ When thinking about addition polymerisation, it is useful to draw the monomer in the shape of an

e.g. **propene:**

$$CH_3-\underset{\underset{\displaystyle H}{|}}{C}=CH_2 \quad \text{as} \quad \underset{\underset{\displaystyle CH_3}{|}\; \underset{\displaystyle H}{|}}{\overset{\overset{\displaystyle H}{|}\; \overset{\displaystyle H}{|}}{C=C}}$$

☐ The repeating unit is:

$$-\underset{\underset{\displaystyle CH_3}{|}\; \underset{\displaystyle H}{|}}{\overset{\overset{\displaystyle H}{|}\; \overset{\displaystyle H}{|}}{C-C}}-$$

☐ Showing three repeating units of the polymer gives:

$$\underset{\underset{\displaystyle CH_3}{|}\; \underset{\displaystyle H}{|}}{\overset{\overset{\displaystyle H}{|}\; \overset{\displaystyle H}{|}}{C=C}} + \underset{\underset{\displaystyle CH_3}{|}\; \underset{\displaystyle H}{|}}{\overset{\overset{\displaystyle H}{|}\; \overset{\displaystyle H}{|}}{C=C}} + \underset{\underset{\displaystyle CH_3}{|}\; \underset{\displaystyle H}{|}}{\overset{\overset{\displaystyle H}{|}\; \overset{\displaystyle H}{|}}{C=C}} \longrightarrow -\underset{\underset{\displaystyle CH_3}{|}\; \underset{\displaystyle H}{|}}{\overset{\overset{\displaystyle H}{|}\; \overset{\displaystyle H}{|}}{C-C}}\underset{\underset{\displaystyle CH_3}{|}\; \underset{\displaystyle H}{|}}{\overset{\overset{\displaystyle H}{|}\; \overset{\displaystyle H}{|}}{C-C}}\underset{\underset{\displaystyle CH_3}{|}\; \underset{\displaystyle H}{|}}{\overset{\overset{\displaystyle H}{|}\; \overset{\displaystyle H}{|}}{C-C}}-$$

propene   **poly(propene)**

Condensation polymers

☐ Esters are formed by the joining together of alcohol and carboxylic acid molecules.

e.g. the reaction between ethanoic acid and methanol can be represented:

acid: ethanoic acid   **alcohol: methanol**

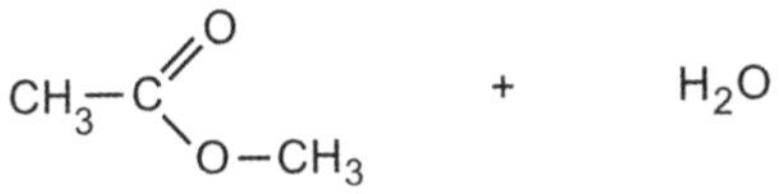

+ H_2O

ester: **methyl ethanoate**

☐ This kind of reaction is called a **condensation** reaction (since two reactants join up with the elimination of two hydrogens and an oxygen to make water).

☐ Polymeric esters (polyesters) are formed by **condensation polymerisation** from alcohols with two hydroxyl groups, –OH, one at either end of the molecules and carboxylic acids with two carboxyl groups, one at either end of the molecules.

$$-\overset{\overset{\displaystyle O}{\|}}{C}-OH$$

☐ This means that the polyester molecules can continue to grow in both directions with many ester linkages.

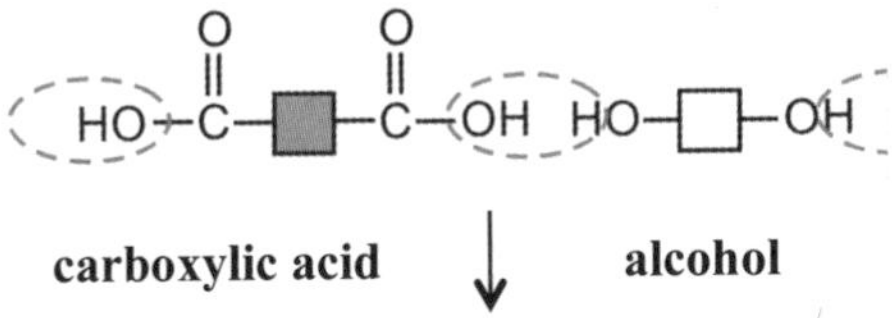

carboxylic acid   ↓   **alcohol**

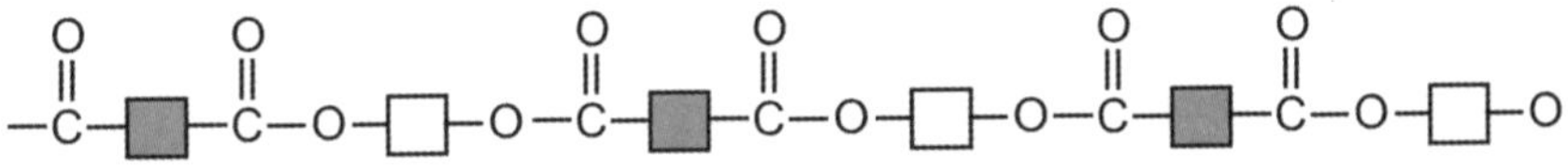

where 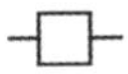 –☐– and –■– represent different arrangements of carbon and hydrogen atoms.

☐ The repeating unit is based on one acid and one alcohol molecule.

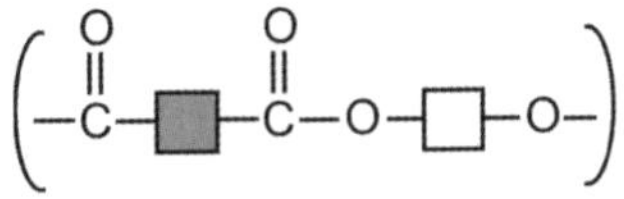

from acid   **from alcohol**

Natural polymers

☐ Many addition and condensation polymers are made by the chemical industry; however, polymers are found in nature in both plants and animals.

☐ Rubber is a natural addition polymer; it has been harvested from trees in Central and South America for hundreds of years.

☐ Recently, scientists have been very successful in making their own versions of rubber to make it stronger and more durable,

e.g. in the manufacture of tyres.

☐ Starch is a natural condensation polymer made from glucose in plants.

☐ Glucose molecules can be represented: HO—[G]—OH

☐ Many glucose molecules can join together by the elimination of the atoms to make water.

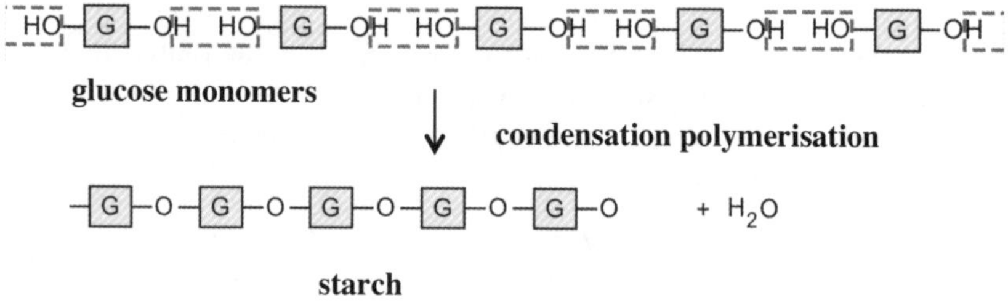

HO—[G]—OH HO—[G]—OH HO—[G]—OH HO—[G]—OH HO—[G]—OH

glucose monomers

↓   **condensation polymerisation**

—[G]—O—[G]—O—[G]—O—[G]—O—[G]—O   + H_2O

starch

☐ Having eaten starchy foods, the reverse process supplies us with the glucose we need for energy.

☐ **Cellulose** is another natural condensation polymer made from glucose; cotton fibres are mainly cellulose.

8 Fertilisers

Important compounds

☐ Much of our food comes from plants; more efficient growth of plants requires the use of **fertilisers**; these are compounds used to restore essential elements to the ground.

☐ The three main elements that are needed by plants are **nitrogen**, **phosphorus** and **potassium**.

☐ Fertilisers must be soluble in water so that they can be taken in by plants through the roots.

☐ However, fertilisers that are very soluble in water can be washed away from the ground by rain-water into rivers and lochs and this can lead to growth of water-plants that are harmful to fish-life.

☐ **Synthetic fertilisers** are made by the chemical industry; those containing nitrogen are made by neutralisation reactions using ammonia or nitric acid.

☐ Many synthetic fertilisers are labelled with an **NPK** analysis; the three numbers correspond to the composition by weight of nitrogen (**N**), phosphorus (**P**) and potassium (**K**) in the fertiliser.

☐ **Natural fertilisers** come from the remains of plants and animals,

   e.g. compost, manure and bone meal.

The industrial manufacture of ammonia

☐ Ammonia is the name given to nitrogen hydride, NH_3.

☐ At room temperature, ammonia is a gas; on cooling the gas liquefies at -33 °C.

☐ In the manufacture of nitrogen fertilisers, ammonia is made and then converted to solid ammonium compounds by the reaction with acids,

   e.g. **ammonia + nitric acid $\longrightarrow$ ammonium nitrate**

☐ The industrial manufacture of ammonia is known as the **Haber Process**.

$$N_2\,(g) \quad + \quad 3H_2\,(g) \quad \rightleftharpoons \quad 2NH_3\,(g)$$

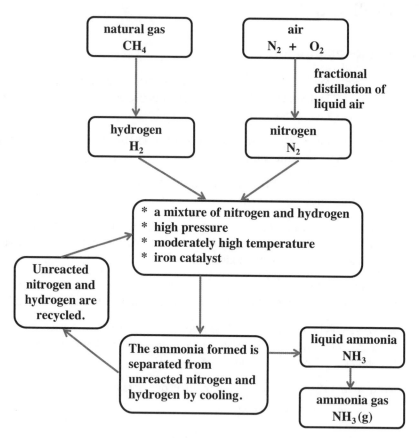

☐ The ⇌ sign indicates that the reaction is reversible; this means that not all the hydrogen and nitrogen are converted to ammonia.

☐ The higher the temperature, the faster the rate but the lower the conversion to ammonia (yield) … so a moderately high temperature is used.

☐ High pressure favours a high yield of ammonia but very high pressures are costly to achieve.

The catalytic oxidation of ammonia

☐ Nitric acid is also used in the industrial manufacture of fertilisers; this acid is formed when nitrogen dioxide dissolves in a mixture of water and oxygen.

☐ Nitrogen and oxygen can be obtained from the air; however, nitrogen is not a very reactive gas due to the energy required to break the triple bonds in the molecules and only combines with oxygen in the presence of a spark,

e.g. during lightning conditions; at the spark-plugs in car engines.

$$N_2 \text{ (g)} \quad + \quad 2O_2 \text{ (g)} \quad \longrightarrow \quad 2NO_2 \text{ (g)}$$

☐ Due to the energy involved, this is **not** an economical route to nitric acid.

☐ The industrial manufacture of nitric acid is by the catalytic oxidation of ammonia, a route known as the **Ostwald Process**.

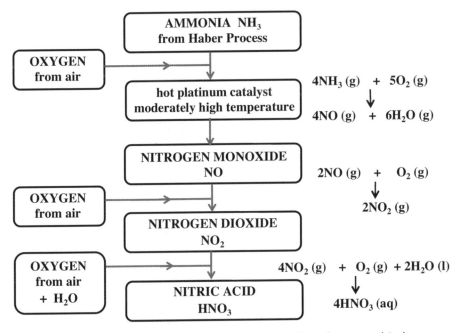

☐ Since the reaction is exothermic (heat is given out) there is no need to keep heating once the reaction has started.

☐ As with the Haber Process, the higher the temperature the faster the rate of the reaction but the lower the yield ... so a moderately high temperature is used.

☐ In the manufacture of nitrogen fertilisers, nitric acid is converted to solid **nitrate** compounds by the reaction with alkalis.

e.g. **nitric acid + potassium hydroxide $\longrightarrow$ potassium nitrate + water**

The percentage composition (by mass)

☐ This is the percentage (by mass) of each element in a compound.

Example 1: Calculate the percentage composition (by mass) of ammonia.

Step 1	Formula	NH_3
Step 2	Formula mass	$14 + (1 \times 3) = 17$
Step 3(a)	% by mass of nitrogen	$\dfrac{\text{mass of nitrogen}}{\text{formula mass of ammonia}} \times 100$

$$\frac{14 \times 100}{17} = \textbf{82.4 \%}$$

Step 3(b)	% by mass of hydrogen	$\dfrac{\text{mass of hydrogen}}{\text{formula mass of ammonia}} \times 100$

$$\frac{3 \times 100}{17} = \textbf{17.6 \%}$$

Example 2: Calculate the percentage of sulphur in ammonium sulphate,

Step 1	Formula	$(NH_4)_2SO_4$
Step 2	Formula mass	$(14+4) \times 2 + 32 + (16 \times 4) = 132$
Step 3	% by mass of sulphur	$\dfrac{\text{mass of sulphur}}{\text{formula mass of ammonium sulphate}} \times 100$

$$\frac{32 \times 100}{132} = \textbf{24\%}$$

For this kind of calculation, an equation is given in the Data Booklet:

$$\% \text{ by mass} = \frac{m}{GFM} \times 100$$

Note that it is not necessary to express the mass of the element and the formula mass in grams (GFM); as in the above method, the mass of the element and the formula mass can be based on relative atomic masses.

---

9 Radioactivity

Atomic structure

☐ The three sub-atomic particles are protons, neutrons and electrons.

Particle	Proton	Neutron	Electron
Symbol	^1_1p	^1_0n	$^0_{-1}e$
Mass	1 amu	1 amu	almost zero
Charge	+	no charge	−
Location	nucleus	nucleus	outside nucleus

☐ The number of protons in the nucleus of an atom of an element is known as the **atomic number**; the **mass number** is the total number of protons and neutrons in the nucleus.

☐ This atomic number and the mass number can be written with the symbol of the element: **Mass number - 35** / **Atomic number - 17** Cl

☐ The mass number can also be written after the name of the element, *e.g. lead-206 has a mass number of 206.*

☐ **Isotopes** are atoms of the one element with different numbers of neutrons.

Formation of elements and background radiation

☐ All naturally occurring elements, including those found in our bodies, have been created in the stars from hydrogen and helium.

☐ The temperature and pressure in the stars is so great that the nuclei of atoms of hydrogen and helium can fuse together to form heavier nuclei, releasing vast quantities of energy; this process is called **nuclear fusion**.

☐ The nuclei of some isotopes are stable; other isotopes have unstable nuclei, i.e. they spontaneously break up (**decay**) with the emission of radiation; this 'happening' is known as **radioactivity**.

☐ **Radioisotopes** are isotopes that are radioactive.

☐ In the radioactive decay process, changes take place in the nuclei of the radioisotopes; this is quite unlike ordinary chemical reactions where the nuclei remain intact and only the outer electrons are involved in the chemical changes.

☐ The radiation that is all around is known as **background radiation**; this varies from place to place.

☐ Natural radiation comes from space (cosmic radiation).

☐ Artificial radiation is a result of human activity,

e.g. the use of radioisotopes in medicine and in nuclear reactors.

☐ Accidents in nuclear power stations can lead to greatly increased levels of background radiation,

e.g. at Chernobyl in Ukraine in 1986 and more recently at Fukushima in Japan following an earthquake and tsunami in 2011.

Radioactivity

☐ Radioisotopes have unstable nuclei, i.e. they spontaneously break up (decay).

☐ The stability of an isotope depends on the relative numbers of protons and neutrons in its nucleus.

☐ The lighter stable nuclei have approximately equal numbers of neutrons and protons but as the nuclei become heavier, the number of neutrons increases more rapidly than the number of protons.

☐ The increase in the neutron to proton ratio with increasing atomic number is due to the neutrons playing a role in dampening the repulsive forces between the protons and thus preventing the nucleus from flying apart.

☐ The **band of stability** shows the neutron to proton ratio in stable isotopes for different elements.

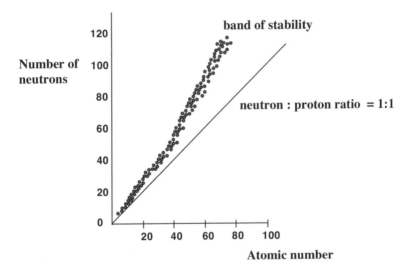

☐ Radioactivity results from the nuclei of unstable isotopes spontaneously disintegrating (decaying) with the emission of radiation.

☐ Radioactive decay alters the neutron to proton ratio with the release of energy and the process continues until the unstable radioactive nuclei form stable nuclei, i.e. nuclei with neutron to proton ratios that lie inside the stability band.

The nature and properties of radiation

☐ **Alpha** (α) and **beta** (β) radiations are made up of particles.

☐ The particles that make up alpha radiation are helium nuclei, i.e. made up of two protons and two neutrons with a mass of 4 amu.

☐ An alpha particle can be represented $_2^4\text{He}^{2+}$.

☐ The particles that make up beta radiation are high energy electrons that are formed in the nucleus when neutrons break up.

$$_0^1\text{n} \longrightarrow {}_1^1\text{p} + {}_{-1}^0\text{e}$$

☐ A beta particle can be represented $_{-1}^0\text{e}$.

☐ A beta particle has almost no mass.

☐ **Gamma** (γ) radiation consists of electromagnetic waves.

☐ Gamma radiation has zero mass and no charge.

Radiation	Alpha	Beta	Gamma
Symbol	α	β	γ
Mass	4 amu	almost zero	zero
Charge	2+	–	zero

☐ The three different types of radiation behave differently in an electric field.

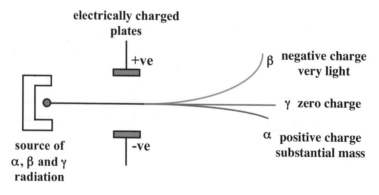

☐ Alpha, beta and gamma radiations also have different penetrating powers.

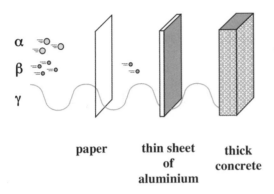

paper   **thin sheet of aluminium**   **thick concrete**

Nuclear reactions

☐ When radioactive atoms disintegrate the changes that take place in the nuclei depend on the type of radiation emitted.

☐ A change in the nucleus can be written in the form of a **nuclear equation**.

☐ In nuclear equations the total mass number on the left hand side of the equation is equal to the total mass number on the right hand side; the same is true for the atomic number.

(a) Alpha decay

☐ When a nucleus emits an alpha particle its atomic number will decrease by two (loss of two protons) and its mass number will decrease by four (loss of two protons and two neutrons).

Example: **Write the nuclear equation for the α-decay of radon-222.**

Mass number	222	$\longrightarrow$	218	+	4
	$^{222}_{86}\text{Rn}$	$\longrightarrow$	$^{218}_{84}\text{Po}$	+	$^{4}_{2}\text{He}^{2+}$
Atomic number	86	$\longrightarrow$	84	+	2

(b) Beta decay

☐ As a result of beta decay, the atomic number of the nucleus will increase by one but the mass number will be unchanged.

Example: **Write the nuclear equation for the β-decay of radium-228.**

Mass number	228	$\longrightarrow$	228	+	0

$$^{228}_{88}\text{Ra} \longrightarrow \, ^{228}_{89}\text{Ac} + \, ^{0}_{-1}\text{e}$$

Atomic number	88	$\longrightarrow$	89	+	-1

(c) Gamma decay

☐ Since gamma rays have no mass and no charge, their emission will have no effect on the mass number and the atomic number of the radioisotope.

Artificial radioisotopes

☐ Artificial radioisotopes are produced by bombarding atoms with particles,

e.g. 'firing' alpha particles at atoms of aluminium-27 results in the formation of phosphorus-30 atoms with the emission of neutrons.

$$^{27}_{13}\text{Al} + \, ^{4}_{2}\alpha \longrightarrow \, ^{30}_{15}\text{P} + \, ^{1}_{0}\text{n}$$

☐ When the particles combine with the nuclei of the bombarded atoms they are said to be **captured**,

e.g. neutron capture can occur when neutrons are used as the bombarding particles.

$$^{59}_{27}\text{Co} + \, ^{1}_{0}\text{n} \longrightarrow \, ^{60}_{27}\text{Co}$$

☐ Again, the total mass numbers and total atomic numbers on both sides of the equation are equal.

Half-life

☐ In a radioisotope, not all the atoms decay at the same time; although the disintegration of the nuclei is completely random the decay curves for all radioisotopes have a similar shape.

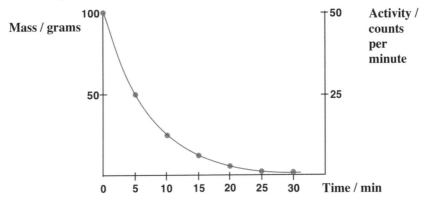

☐ The time for a radioisotope to half its initial activity is known as the **half-life** (often abbreviated to $t_{1/2}$); it is also the time it takes for half the radioactive atoms initially present to disintegrate or the mass of the original radioisotope to halve.

☐ While the activity of a radioisotope depends on the mass present, the half-life of a radioisotope is independent of this, i.e. the time for half of a 1 kg sample of a radioisotope to decay is the same as the time for half of a 1 g sample of the same radioisotope to decay.

☐ The half-life of a radioisotope is the same no matter whether the radioisotope is present as atoms of the element or as ions in a compound,

e.g. the half-life of lead-206 in the element is the same as the half-life of lead-206 in PbCl₂.

☐ This is because the formation of a compound involves electrons and not the nucleus of an atom, i.e. radioactive decay is a nuclear reaction and the nucleus of an atom and its corresponding ion are identical.

☐ The half-life is **not** affected by changes in temperature or pressure or by the presence of a catalyst.

☐ Some radioisotopes have a very short half-life, others have very long half-lives,

e.g. radon-220 has a half-life of 55 s; uranium-238 has a half-life of 4.51 x 10⁹ years).

□ The change in activity and mass of a radioisotope with a half-life of **x** days and starting mass **y** g is shown in the table.

Number of half lives	0	1	2	3
Time elapsed / days	0	x	2x	3x
Fraction of the original activity left	1	$^1/_2$	$^1/_4$	$^1/_8$
Mass of original radioisotope left / g	y	$^1/_2\,y$	$^1/_4\,y$	$^1/_8\,y$

Example 1: A radioisotope of phosphorus has a half-life of 14 days. A sample of the radioisotope has a mass of 80 g.

Calculate the remaining mass of the sample of the radioisotope after 56 days.

Time passed　　　　　　　 =　　56 days
Half-life　　　　　　　　　 =　　14 days
Number of half-life periods　 =　　4

Time	Mass
0	80 g
1 x $t_{1/2}$	40 g
2 x $t_{1/2}$	20 g
3 x $t_{1/2}$	10 g
4 x $t_{1/2}$	**5 g**

Example 2: The initial radioactivity of a sample of a radioisotope was 100 counts/minute.

If the activity fell to 25 counts/minute in 24 days, calculate the half-life of the radioisotope.

Time	Activity in counts/minute
0	100
1 x $t_{1/2}$	50
2 x $t_{1/2}$	25

2 x $t_{1/2}$　　 =　　24 days
$t_{1/2}$　　　　 =　　**12 days**

Example 3: A radioisotope has a half-life of 7 s.

Calculate how long it will take for 48 g of the radioisotope to decay to leave 6 g.

Time	Mass
0	48 g
$t_{1/2}$	24 g
$2 \times t_{1/2}$	12 g
$3 \times t_{1/2}$	6 g

$$t_{1/2} = 7\text{ s}$$
$$3 \times t_{1/2} = \mathbf{21\text{ s}}$$

Uses of radioisotopes

☐ The use of a radioisotope depends on its penetrating power and its half-life.

(a) In scientific research

(i) As a tracer

☐ Scientists can label atoms in molecules by making a proportion of the molecules from a radioactive isotope; the path of an atom from one molecule to another in biological processes and chemical reactions can be followed using molecules with isotopic labels (tracers).

(ii) Carbon dating

☐ Atmospheric carbon dioxide contains the radioisotope carbon-14, formed when cosmic ray neutrons bombard molecules of nitrogen.

☐ Since the rate of decay is the same as the rate of formation there is a constant level of carbon-14 in the atmosphere.

☐ Plants and animals have this same proportion as long as they are living but once they die, the level of radioactivity will decrease; the proportion of carbon-14 left in a sample of carbon taken from the plant or animal can be used with the half-life of carbon-14 (5730 years) to determine the age of the sample.

Example: Carbon from a wooden beam in an ancient tomb has an activity of 3.75 counts per minute per gram of carbon. New wood has an activity of 15.0 counts per minute per gram of carbon.

Calculate the age of the beam.

Two half-lives must have passed to reduce the activity from 15.0 to 3.75 counts

$$15.00 \longrightarrow 7.5 \longrightarrow 3.75 \text{ counts per minute}$$

i.e. two half lives

and so the wooden beam must be 2 x 5730, i.e. **11 460 years** old.

(b) In medicine

☐ Gamma emitters with a short half-life are used; the radiation has to be able to penetrate body cells and the half-life must be relatively short to minimise the harmful effects of unwanted cell damage,

e.g. yttrium-90 is used to kill cancer cells; cobalt-60 is used in radiotherapy treatment.

☐ In some cases, the radioisotope is ingested by the patient, i.e. taken inside the body by swallowing or injection,

e.g. technetium-89 is used in imaging of heart and thyroid conditions.

(c) In industry

☐ Radioisotopes are used in industry to detect flaws in metal pipes and to control the thickness of sheets in a production line.

☐ Industrial radioisotopes tend to have a long half-life to prolong working use.

10 Chemical analysis

☐ Chemists monitor our environment through the use a variety of analytical techniques to ensure that it remains healthy and safe and that pollution is tackled as it arises.

☐ Although modern analytical chemistry makes use of sophisticated instrumentation, the roots of analytical chemistry and some of the principles used in modern instruments come from traditional techniques many of which are still used today.

(a) Qualitative analysis

☐ **Qualitative analysis** gives an indication of the presence or absence of particular atoms, ions or molecules in a sample,

e.g. chemical tests can be considered to be examples of qualitative analysis.

(i) Flame tests

☐ Metals (both as atoms in the element and ions in a compound) change the colour of a flame when they are heated in it; different metals give different colours to the flame, so flame tests can be used to identify the presence of a particular metal in a sample (see page 6 of the Data Booklet).

e.g. the characteristic flame colour for sodium is yellow.

(ii) Detecting acids and alkalis using litmus paper

☐ Litmus paper turns red in the presence of acids and blue in the presence of alkalis, and so can be used to find out if water samples are acidic or alkaline.

(iii) Detection of halide ions

☐ Silver nitrate solution can be used to detect halide ions (ions of group 7 elements) since an insoluble compound (a precipitate) is formed; the absence of a precipitate shows that halide ions are not in a sample.

☐ A positive result to the test does not indicate which halide ion is present … the ions of all the Group 7 elements (as well as some other ions) form a precipitate with silver nitrate solution; however, the differences in the colour of the precipitates give a clue to the particular halide ion present.

(b) Quantitative analysis

☐ **Quantitative analysis**, as the name suggests, is related to quantities,

e.g. the mass or concentration of particular atoms, ions or molecules in a sample.

(i) pH measurement

☐ The acidity or alkalinity of water samples can be found by pH measurement; the lower below pH 7, the greater the acidity;   the higher above pH 7 the greater the alkalinity.

☐ Since the pH number is related to the concentration of aqueous hydrogen ions, H^+ (aq) , and hydroxide ions, OH^- (aq), pH measurement is an example of quantitative analysis.

(ii) Volumetric titrations (acid – alkali titrations)

☐ This technique is a more accurate way to find the concentration of aqueous hydrogen ions, H^+ (aq), or hydroxide ions, OH^- (aq), in a sample of water; the neutralisation reaction can be followed using an indicator that changes colour at the end-point (see notes on page 72).

(iii) Measurement of halide ion concentration

☐ If the precipitate obtained from a known volume of a water sample is filtered off, dried and weighed, then the concentration of a halide ion can be found.

Example: When silver nitrate solution is added to 25 cm^3 of a water sample containing chloride ions, 2.87 g of silver chloride is formed.

Calculate the concentration of chloride ions in the sample.

Formula		AgCl
Formula mass		$= 108 + 35.5$ $= 143.5$
Mass of one mole (GFM)		143.5 g

Find the number of moles   no. of moles $= \dfrac{mass}{GFM}$

$$\boxed{n = \dfrac{m}{GFM}}$$

$$= \dfrac{2.87}{143.5} = 0.02 \text{ mol}$$

Calculate concentration   concentration $= \dfrac{no.\ of\ moles}{litres}$

$$\boxed{C = \dfrac{n}{V}}$$

$$= \dfrac{0.02}{0.025} = \textbf{0.8 mol l}^{-1}$$